Staff Development and Continuing Education

CLIP NOTE #18

compiled by

Elizabeth A. Sudduth
Head of Library Technical Services
McGraw-Page Library
Randolph-Macon College
Ashland, Virginia

Lynn W. Livingston
Information Services Librarian
Franklin F. Moore Library
Rider College
Lawrenceville, New Jersey

College Library Information Packet Committee
College Libraries Section
Association of College and Research Libraries
A Division of American Library Association

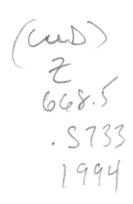

ASSOCIATION OF

COLLEGE

& RESEARCH

LIBRARIES

Published by the Association of College and Research Libraries
A Division of the American Library Association
50 East Huron Street
Chicago, IL 60611-2795
1-800-545-2433

ISBN: 0-8389-7715-4

This publication is printed on recycled, acid-free paper.

Printed in the United States of America.

Table of Contents

CLIP NOTES COMMITTEE

Patricia Smith Butcher
Trenton (NJ) State College

Carol F. Goodson
West Georgia College

Andrea C. Hoffman
Wheelock College

Lawrie Metz
Houghton College

Allen S. Morrill
Kansas City Art Institute

Karen A. Nuckolls
Skidmore College

Introduction

Objective

The College Library Information Packet (CLIP) Notes publishing program, under the auspices of the College Libraries Section of the Association of College and Research Libraries, provides "college and small university libraries with state-of-the-art reviews and current documentation on library practices and procedures of relevance to them" (Morein 226). This CLIP Note provides information on staff development and continuing education programming and policies.

Background

It is apparent that staff development and continuing education for librarians are crucial in this era of rapid technological change and budget constraints (Kong 208). College libraries have responded to these needs by providing ad hoc training, by supporting continuing education programs, by working together to provide regional workshops and programs, and by offering more formal programs for staff and professional development. (For examples of additional staff development policies, see Lipow.)

The purpose of this survey was to collect data and supporting documents on the state of staff development and continuing education in academic libraries for both professional librarians and library paraprofessionals.[1] Taking the broadest possible view of staff development and continuing education, we examined how small and medium size academic libraries were providing such programming in an era of changing technology and tight budgets (Creth 132; for historical background, see Peterson). While many of the libraries participating in the survey did not have written policies, all libraries reported that they developed programming in the library or took advantage of programs

---

[1] A "professional librarian" is defined as a person holding a master's degree in library or information science. A "library paraprofessional" is defined as a library employee who does not have a masters degree in library or information science but who works in a support position with a title such as library assistant, associate, or technical assistant. These positions, as defined, do not include secretaries, bookkeepers, typists, student employees, or professionals in other fields who do not hold a masters degree in library or information science.

offered on campus or those provided by any one of a number of professional organizations or consortia. A number of respondents without written policies at the time of the survey indicated that their library or institution was in the process of developing written policies. Others responded that their libraries were too small to need a written policy (Vondran 136 and other articles in Topics In Personnel Kit #12).

Sample and Procedure

In order to provide a representative sample of college libraries, the compilers utilized groupings established by the Carnegie Foundation for the Advancement of Teaching. Institutions from two Carnegie list groups, "Comprehensive Universities and Colleges I" and "Liberal Arts Colleges I," who had previously agreed to participate in CLIP Note surveys, comprised the sample.

Upon approval of the survey instrument by the CLIP Note Committee, a questionnaire was distributed to 254 college and university libraries in February 1993. Follow-up postcards and duplicate surveys (when requested) were subsequently distributed. A total of 157 surveys or 62% were returned. The length of the survey, which included 51 questions, probably had a negative effect on the response rate.

Findings

General Characteristics
(Questions 1-11)

Responses were received from 139 private and 18 public academic libraries. The "average" respondent was a library director at a small to medium-sized private liberal arts college employing six professional librarians, including four with faculty status, and an average total staff size of 15 full-time equivalents.

Staff Development and Continuing Education Policies (Questions 12-22)

Only 12% of the responding libraries had written library policies covering any aspect of staff development, including professional development, staff training, or continuing education. Of the 19 libraries that had written policies, the majority had library policies covering only professional librarians. Thirty-one libraries reported that some library employees were covered by an institutional policy. Most of the libraries with written policies had written and updated the policies within the last ten years.

The eighteen public academic libraries responding accounted for 5 of the library staff development policies. Another 7 public academic libraries had institutional policies covering staff development.

Thirty-seven percent of responding libraries with written library staff development policies employed professional librarians who were reviewed via the tenure process. Thirty-five percent of responding libraries covered institutional staff development policies employed professional librarians who were reviewed via the tenure process.

It would be worthwhile to examine the relationship between an institution's funding, whether public or private, and the existence of staff development policies and financial support for staff development. An in-depth examination of the relationship between an institution's use of the tenure review process for librarians and funding and support for staff development would also be worthy of further study.

Budget/Expenditures for Staff Development Programming (Questions 23-36)

Staff development activities were funded through the library's budget for 51% of the respondents. Thirty-seven percent of the respondents indicated that staff development activities were funded at the institutional level. Just under half of all libraries responding (47%) had a mix of library and institutional funds available for staff development activities. In many cases the funds that were available were in the "travel" line of the library's budget. Several libraries commented that "travel" was loosely interpreted to include costs associated with staff development and training. Some libraries noted that funds not expended in other budget categories are applied to cover staff development activities.

Budgeted funds were used for both professionals and paraprofessionals to attend conferences and workshops as well as for continuing education. Substantially fewer libraries provided for continuing education not directly related to the job in their budgets. Five percent of the respondents did not provide funds in their budgets for professional librarians to attend conferences, workshops, or participate in continuing education activities. Eleven percent of the respondents did not provide funds in their budgets for library paraprofessionals to attend conferences, workshops, or participate in continuing education activities. In general, libraries who had larger staff development budgets provided more funds for library paraprofessionals.

Twenty-six percent of the respondents indicated that their library budgeted less than $1,000 for staff development, 41% of the respondents budgeted between $1,001 and $5,000, and 17% of the respondents budgeted between $5,001 and $10,000. Only 4% of the libraries budgeted over $10,000. Most libraries (72%) indicated that three-fourths or more of their staff development budget was used for professional librarians.

In-house programming can be a significant part of a staff development plan. Only 12% of the respondents' library budgets included a line for programming costs such as speakers' fees and materials. From the lists of programming and descriptions provided it is evident that many libraries have been using staff as speakers. Often these staff members received training at a workshop and then presented a program to their colleagues in their library.

Twelve percent of the libraries responded that they had utilized grant funding to support staff development programming. Sources of grants included: a staff development component in a Title III grant, Friends of the Library groups, consortial grants, and grants from foundations.

Over 60% of the respondents' libraries have provided both paid and unpaid leave to professional librarians participating in training, staff development, or continuing education. At the same time, over 60% of the libraries responded that they did not provide paid or unpaid leave for library paraprofessionals. One notable exception was the case of a library paraprofessional working on a bachelor's degree or a master's degree in library or information science.

Staff Development Programming and Coordination
(Questions 37-47)

Only 24% of libraries surveyed offered a formal orientation program for both newly hired professionals and for paraprofessionals. An additional 6% provide structured orientation for either new library professionals or paraprofessionals.

Internships were offered in conjunction with library schools (5%), and one college provided paid library school internships in cataloging and archives management. Mentoring programs (8%) ranged from information and guidance on promotion, tenure, and publication to institution-wide mentoring (for faculty) or state-wide mentoring (for librarians).

Programming needs assessments (developed in some form by 19% of respondents) have been conducted through focus groups, at staff retreats, as part of a campus-wide survey, by ACRL chapters, and by regional consortia. The greatest demand was for computer skills training and workshops on online systems and electronic databases. Management and human resources skills were also frequent requests. Library programming of particular interest to the compilers of this <u>CLIP Note</u> included:

        -writing a new library proposal
        -explaining job to others
        -conducting successful meetings
        -BI for paraprofessionals
        -paraprofessional visits to neighboring libraries

(See lists under questions 43 and 44 of survey instrument results for more detail.)

Many libraries conducted in-service training related to departmental responsibilities for all staff; three held annual retreats. One library held a paraprofessional retreat yearly. Fewer than 8% of respondents asked for a written evaluation of staff development programming.

The Library Director was responsible for staff development planning in 59% of the libraries surveyed. In another 16% the responsibility for staff development planning fell on Department Heads. Only 7% of college libraries surveyed had a staff development committee.

Consortial/Regional Programming and Exchanges (Questions 48-51)

Most college libraries (75%) participated in consortial or regional programming. Only 11% of respondents listed in-library programming that was broader in focus than departmental or job-related training. Staff development was part of a policy or mission statement for at least 32% of the organizations. A number of respondents indicated uncertainty as to whether their consortium had a formal commitment to staff development. Programming for regions varied from "a wide variety of workshops, discussion groups, and conferences" to "none." Only two libraries were involved in organized, on-going exchange programs, although another fourteen have had someone participate in such an exchange in the past.

Conclusion

Results indicate that the small and medium sized academic libraries surveyed are actively engaged in on- and off- site staff development programming. However, most libraries lack written policies and appear to be using a variety of resources outside their library budgets.

Only 12% of the college libraries surveyed had a written library policy covering any aspect of library staff development. Even at the institutional level, only 21% of the college libraries surveyed had written policies on staff development. Most of the library staff development policies were written or revised during the last 10 years. A number of libraries indicated that they were in the process of beginning to draft documentation.

Fifty-one percent of the responding libraries budgeted for staff development as a separate line item within their budgets. One third of these libraries allocated less than $1,000 annually for library staff development. Libraries surveyed are using institutional funding and/or grants from a variety of sources to augment funds in their own budgets. Most libraries mentioned taking advantage of consortial programming. A number of libraries specifically cited using the "train the trainer approach," sending one staff member to a workshop or conference to return and develop an in-house version, as a means of containing costs.

It is our belief that more small and medium sized academic libraries will be formalizing their staff development programs as they need to justify expenditures and as they more fully appreciate staff development as an investment. We recommend that this survey be replicated in five years.

Works Cited

Carnegie Foundation for the Advancement of Teaching. A Classification of Institutions of Higher Education. Princeton, N.J.: Carnegie Foundation for the Advancement of Teaching, 1987.

Creth, Sheila D. "Staff Development: Where Do We Go From Here?" Library Administration & Management 4, (Summer 1990): 131-132.

Kong, Leslie M. and Goodfellow, R.A.H. "Charting a Career Path in the Information Professions." College and Research Libraries 49 (May 1988): 207-216.

Lipow, Anne Grodzind and Carver, Deborah S., eds. Staff Development: A Practical Guide. 2nd ed. Chicago: Library Administration and Management Association, American Library Association, 1992.

Morein, Grady. "What is a CLIP Note?" College and Research Library News 46 (May 1985): 226-229.

Peterson, Lorna. Professional Development for College and University Librarians: A Selective Bibliography. Public Administration Series -- Bibliography, no. 1675. Monticello, Ill.: Vance Bibliographies, 1985.

Smith, Kitty, ed. Career Development: Concepts and Strategies (Topics in Personnel Kit, no. 12) Chicago: American Library Association, Office for Library Personnel Resources, 1990.

Vondran, Raymond F. and Person, Ruth J. "Library Education and Professional Practice: Agendas for Partnership." Library Administration and Management 4 (Summer 1990): 133-137.

CLIP Note Survey Results

Staff Development and Continuing Education
A CLIP Note Survey

General Institutional Questions

1. Institution name

   __18__ Public   *157 responses*
   __139__ Private

2. Address

3. Name of respondent

   Please indicate if this is an address or name change

4. Title

5. Telephone number

6. Fax number

7. Electronic mail address

Data for last fiscal year (FY 1991-1992)

8. If your records cover a period other than that of July 1, 1991 - June 30, 1992, please indicate the period used.

9. Number of FTE professional librarians[1]:

   155 responses

   min.   2
   max. 17
   mean 6.119

---

[1] We are defining professional librarians as persons holding a masters degree in library or information science.

10. Number of FTE professional librarians with faculty status:

151 responses

    min.   0
    max. 17
    mean 4.084

11. Total number of FTE library employees:

155 responses

    min.   2
    max. 59.75
    mean 15.142

12. Professional librarians at your institution are:

154 responses

  62 a. faculty who are reviewed via the tenure process
  32 b. faculty who are reviewed via another type of review process, such as a five year review
  51 c. academic professionals or administrative professionals who are reviewed via another type of review process, such as a five year review
  24 d. other - only Head Librarian has faculty status;
                  faculty are reviewed annually;
                  librarians are faculty but are not eligible for tenure;
                  no tenure on campus

Existence of Policy

13. Does your library have a written policy covering any aspect of staff development[2], including professional development, staff training[3] and/or continuing education?

154 responses

  19 a. yes
 135 b. no

---

[2]We are using the phrase "staff development" in the broadest sense to include professional development and development programming for paraprofessionals.

[3]Staff training involves programming devoted to developing a particular task or skill. An example of staff training would be a workshop on how to make labels using a new software package.

14. Please check all of the following which describe the coverage of your
    library's policy:

21 responses

    <u>18</u> a. covers staff development activities for professional librarians
    <u>17</u> b. covers continuing education for professional librarians
    <u>15</u> c. covers training activities for professional librarians
    <u>12</u> d. covers staff development activities for library paraprofessionals[4]
    <u>11</u> e. covers continuing education for library paraprofessionals
    <u>8</u> f. covers training activities for library paraprofessionals

15. When was the library's policy originally written?

    <u>Comments</u>: Dates given: **1974, 1979, 1982-1985, 1988, 1990-1992**

16. When was the library's policy first put into effect?

    <u>Comments</u>: Dates given: **1973-1974, 1979, 1982-1985, 1989-1992**

17. When was the library's policy on development last updated?

    <u>Comments</u>: Dates given: **1973, 1984, 1989-1993**

---

[4] We are defining library paraprofessionals as library employees who do
not have a masters degree in library or information science and who work in
support positions with titles such as library assistant, associate, technical
assistant, etc. Our definition of library paraprofessionals does **not** include
secretaries, bookkeepers, typists, students employees, or professionals in
other fields who do not hold a master's degree in library or information
science.

right

18. Does your institution have a written development policy that includes library employees?

145 responses

<u>31</u> a. yes
<u>114</u> b. no

19. Please check all of the following which describe the coverage of your institution's policy:

31 responses

<u>11</u> a. covers professional librarians only
<u>1</u> b. covers library paraprofessionals only
<u>19</u> c. covers both professional librarians and library paraprofessionals

20. When was your institution's policy originally written?

<u>Comments</u>: Dates given: 1960, 1975, 1980, 1982, 1985, 1989, 1990, 1992

21. When was your institution's policy first put into effect?

<u>Comments</u>: Dates given: 1962, 1975, 1980, 1982, 1985, 1989, 1990, 1992

22. When was your institution's policy last updated?

<u>Comments</u>: Dates given: 1987, 1990-1993

23. Is staff development and/or education included in your library's budget as a separate line item?

155 responses

79 a. yes
76 b. no

24. Is staff development and/or education included in your institution's budget as a separate line item?

153 responses

56 a. yes
54 b. no
43 c. don't know

25. Check below if your library's budget provides funds for professional librarians to:

155 responses

139 a. attend conferences
144 b. attend workshops
119 c. participate in continuing education directly related to job
30 d. participate in continuing education not directly related to job
7 e. none of the above, there is no provision in the library's budget for attending conferences, workshops, or continuing education

26. Check below if your library's budget provides funds for library paraprofessionals to:

151 responses

109 a. attend conferences
126 b. attend workshops
102 c. participate in continuing education directly related to job
14 d. participate in continuing education not directly related to job
16 e. none of the above, there is no provision in the library's budget for attending conferences, workshops, or continuing education

27. How much is budgeted by the library for staff development?

155 responses

18 a. not budgeted
40 b. less than $1,000
36 c. $1,001-$2,500
28 d. $2,501-$5,000
27 e. $5,001-$10,000
6 f. greater than $10,001

28. Of the amount checked above please estimate what percentage is used for professional librarians:

140 responses

11 a. 100%
89 b. 75% - 99%
32 c. 50% - 74%
5 d. 25% - 49%
0 e. 1% - 24%
3 f. 0%

29. The institution offers funding in addition to the library's budget to allow professional librarians to:

149 responses

81 a. attend conferences
72 b. attend workshops
64 c. participate in continuing education directly related to job
19 d. participate in continuing education not directly related to job
52 e. none of the above, the institution does not offer funding in addition to the library's budget for professional librarians to attend conferences, workshops, or participate in continuing education

30. The institution offers funding in addition to the library's budget to allow library paraprofessionals to:

149 responses

27 a. attend conferences
30 b. attend workshops
34 c. participate in continuing education directly related to job
9 d. participate in continuing education not directly related to job
101 e. none of the above, the institution does not offer funding in addition to the library's budget for library paraprofessionals to attend conferences, workshops, or participate in continuing education

Comments: A number of schools added that they offer staff the opportunity to take courses at little or no cost. Most often this benefit relates to courses offered on campus; occasionally, courses at other institutions are covered. Examples cited were the provision for a paraprofessional to obtain a college degree or to take library science courses.

31. Does your library's budget include a line for programming, to cover materials, speaker's fees, etc.?

155 responses

 18 a. yes
137 b. no

32. Has your library secured grant funding to support staff development programming?

154 responses

 19 a. yes
135 b. no

Comments: Sources of funding include: grants from a church organization, consortium, network, Title III, the Richardson Foundation, and the Kellog Foundation.

33. Does your library provide paid leave[5] for professional librarians engaging in training, staff development or continuing education activities?

151 responses

94 a. yes
57 b. no

Comments: In a number of libraries, professional librarians have sabbatical or administrative leave privileges which they use to attend conferences and workshops (one week or longer), to work on research, dissertations, or theses, to take graduate courses, to participate in workshops or programs overseas, and/or to participate in internships.

---

[5] Leave is the release from daily duties that requires formal approval by the library and/or the institutions's administration. A leave involves an extended period of time such as a week, a month, or longer and can be granted with or without pay and benefits.

34. Does your library provide unpaid leave for professional librarians engaging in training, development or continuing education activities?

147 responses

95 a. yes
52 b. no

35. Does your library provide paid leave for library paraprofessionals engaging in training, development or continuing education activities?

151 responses

54 a. yes
97 b. no

36. Does your library provide unpaid leave for library paraprofessionals engaging in training, development or continuing education activities?

148 responses

59 a. yes
89 b. no

Comments: Release time for paraprofessionals to take undergraduate or library school courses is fairly common. Additional details were lacking.

37. Does your library have a formal orientation program for newly hired employees? (A formal program involves a schedule and written materials that are updated when needed.)

156 responses

38 a. yes, for library paraprofessional staff and professional librarians
5 b. yes, for library paraprofessionals only
5 c. yes, for professional librarians only
108 d. no, we have no planned orientation program, each new employee receives an informal ad hoc orientation
2 e. no, we do not conduct any type of orientation for new employees

Comments: 1 in planning process now
1 part of college orientation
2 some periodic formal sessions

38. Is there a provision for continuing training for library
    paraprofessionals?

154 responses

_80_ a. yes, library paraprofessionals attend relevant training sessions in
     their work areas

_51_ b. yes, library paraprofessionals attend sessions available to all
     library paraprofessionals

_78_ c. yes, library paraprofessionals attend various types of relevant
     programming available on campus

_76_ d. yes, library paraprofessionals attend various types of programming
     available regionally

_43_ e. yes, our library cross-trains library paraprofessionals within work
     area

_38_ f. yes, our library cross-trains library paraprofessionals across work
     areas

_30_ g. no, our library's provision for continuing training for library
     paraprofessionals is left to each employee's supervisor

_18_ h. no, our library does not have a plan for continued training of
     library paraprofessionals

39. Does your library have an internship program for new professionals?

155 responses

_7_ a. yes
_148_ b. no

40. Does your library have a mentor program for new professionals?

155 responses

_13_ a. yes
_142_ b. no

Comments:

_1_ Mentor assigned for 1 year of guidance

_3_ Informal arrangement regarding promotion, tenure, publication,
    campus introductions

_1_ Function performed by supervisor

_2_ Institution-wide faculty mentor program includes librarians

_1_ State-wide mentoring program for librarians (IL)

41. Has your library ever conducted a needs/interest survey of all employees to determine what kinds of programming would be useful?

155 responses

  29 a. yes
 126 b. no

Comments:
  4 Through informal discussion
  3 Conducted by region/consortium
  2 Conducted by ACRL Chapter
  2 Campus-wide programming survey
  2 Small group, meets often, no need for survey
  1 A focus-group survey
  1 Once, now out of date

42. How often is a needs/interest survey done?

132 responses

  9 a. at least annually
  6 b. less frequently than annually
 22 c. as need arises
 95 d. never done

Comments:
  2 As part of the evaluation process
  1 In conjunction with staff development activities

43. What types of programming have resulted from the needs/interest survey?

Comments:
 12 Introduction to new software packages
  7 Online systems, electronic databases
  7 Library areas: Government Documents, Audio-Visual, disaster plans the teaching/learning process
  5 Management skills: student training, team building, TQM, time management, conflict resolution
  5 Human resources: customer service, multicultural communication, sexual harassment, stress
  2 Tours of other libraries
  2 Day of inservice, 3-day consultant-led workshop
  2 Cross-training between departments

44. What types of programming have been conducted at your library in the last year and what library departments or work areas were involved?

Comments:
Several libraries indicated that they hold annual or semi-annual retreats where the following topics were covered: strategic planning, organizational development (with a psychologist), TQM in libraries, teambuilding and goal setting, "Our library in the year 2000", Covey's Seven Habits of Highly Effective People.

Most libraries conducted in-service programming related to departmental responsibilities. Programming for all staff included such topics as: automated systems, new technologies, the Internet, customer service, positive communication, wellness workshops, time management, and the evaluation process.

45. Does your library provide for the written evaluation of staff development programming?

140 responses

_11_ a. yes
129 b. no

Coordination of staff development programming

46. Who is responsible for coordinating staff development programs in your library?

150 responses

_89_ a. director
__ b. library personnel officer
_25_ c. division or department heads
_10_ d. staff development committee
_44_ e. no single individual or committee designated
_6_ f. other: director and one professional librarian, Staff Development Committee Chair, Reference Librarian

47. If a committee coordinates staff development in your library describe its composition.

Comments: Librarians and support staff (9), 4 librarians (1), director and 3 department heads (1), Staff Development component of the Human Resources Committee (1).

Consortial or Regional Programming and Exchanges

48. Does your library participate in a consortium or regional group that provides staff development programming?

153 responses

__116__ a. yes
__37__ b. no

49. Does the consortium or regional group address staff development in a policy or mission statement?

124 responses

__40__ a. yes
__84__ b. no

50. What programming has the consortium or regional group provided within the last year?

Comments: workshops: use of OCLC products, Internet, CD-Rom databases, document delivery services, American Disabilities Act, copyright, preservation, Total Quality Management, and supervising student employees.

51. Does your library have an exchange program for professionals or library paraprofessionals?

148 responses

__3__ a. yes, our library participates in a formal exchange program
__15__ b. no, but professionals from our library have participated in an exchange
__4__ c. no, but library paraprofessionals from our library have participated in an exchange
__126__ d. no, we have not participated in any type of exchange

Library Staff Development Documents

ALVERNO COLLEGE LIBRARY MEDIA CENTER
STAFF DEVELOPMENT AND CONTINUING EDUCATION POLICY

Alverno College Library Media Center supports the Alverno College Mission and
ementation Goals. The mission and goals related to staff development and
nuing education are:

Mission

> Creating a community of learning: the common purpose that
> gathers everyone at Alverno is the pursuit of knowledge and the
> development of students' abilities.

Implementing the Mission

> We implement this philosophy by learning its responsibilities,
> rising to its challenge and taking on leadership for change

> We recognize that we share equal responsibility for quality performance

> We improve constantly every process for planning, production and service

> We recognize the importance of effective on-the-job training

> We recognize the need for a vigorous program of education and self-
> improvement

The Library Media Center supports the above stated Mission and Implementation
by:

Encouraging and allowing all professional, paraprofessional, and clerical staff to
attend on campus and off-campus courses, workshops, conferences, seminars,
programs, etc. relevant to their areas of work and/or related to personal
and professional growth

Supporting financially the tuition or registration fees for relevant continuing
education and staff development programs, travel to those programs, and lodging
and meal costs, if needed

Supporting release time from job responsibilities, if needed and as negotiated with
the individual's supervisor and the library director

ollege supports the above stated Mission and Implementation Goals by:

Offering tuition reimbursement for classes offered at the College for those
yees   employed 20 hours or more per week and who have been employed for one
r longer

Offering on-campus continuous improvement and staff development workshops for employees

Supporting effective on-the-job training and training guidelines for supervisors through the College Training Committee

ANDREWS LIBRARY STAFF DEVELOPMENT GUIDELINES

Purpose: To provide clear, albeit broadly-defined guidelines for the entire library staff (hourly, salaried, and faculty) on the types of staff development activities that are both appropriate and encouraged, as well as methods for planning and budgeting or obtaining funds for those activities.

General Overall Guidelines: It is assumed that each individual staff member is ultimately responsible for deciding on and planning for appropriate staff development activities for his/her needs. If an individual is unsure of which consortium activities, workshops, conferences, etc. which might be appropriate, that individual is encouraged to consult with a supervisor, colleague, and/or other library staff member for suggestions. Planning should include both budgeting for and planning ahead of time for the individual's areas of responsibility to either be covered in his/her absence; or, when coverage is impossible, an individual's absence should be made known to his/her supervisor, the library director, and appropriate "others" on campus who will be affected during his/her absence. Specific applications of these guidelines in respect to attendance at particular conferences or activities are published from time to time by the director of the library. Supervisors or others on the library staff are asked to support other staff members' staff development activities by covering for those individuals during their absence.

Budgeting/Funding Sources for Staff Development Activities: It is assumed that all staff development activities, except in extenuating circumstances and where funds are available elsewhere on campus, will be paid for out of the library's *Travel & Entertainment (7021)* budget line. In the case of the library faculty conference benefit, appropriate funds are to be obtained from the Vice President for Academic Affairs office. In addition, the library faculty are encouraged to request faculty development funds through the Dean of Faculty's office when appropriate, in order to help reserve funds in the *7021* budget line for others. When planning staff development activities, individuals are asked to be reasonable in their requests (e.g., try to plan for workshops that are held within driving distance and are low in cost, if possible). An individual may on occasion expect to be denied a request due to lack of funds or planning on the part of the individual.

For annual budgeting purposes, staff development activities should be anticipated by the individual/department and included in departmental budget requests each year. Included should be expenses related to transportation (mileage/travel expenses), lodging, meals, parking, and registration fees, as appropriate. Dues for individual memberships in professional associations and consortia are the responsibility of the individual.

If an individual knows of or has access to other sources of funding (e.g., grants through professional associations), the individual is encouraged to pursue such funding.

When small group workshops/meetings are hosted at Wooster (e.g., NEOMARL committee meeting), it is expected that the library's *Travel & Entertainment* budget line will cover the cost of breaks. Ordinarily, when lunch is a part of a small group workshop/meeting, it is assumed that costs will be recovered via fees for attendance. When large group workshops/meetings are hosted at Wooster, it is assumed that costs will be recovered either via fees for attendance, funds from the association involved, and/or other means of funding. Related paper/copying and mailing costs will be absorbed into other appropriate library budget lines.

Consortium Activities: It is assumed that all of the library staff are affected by and may need to participate in the activities pursued by the variety of consortia of which our library/institution/individual on the staff is a member (e.g., NEOMARL, NOTSL, GLCA, etc.). Contact with other institutions in the library field is essential in order to keep our skills/knowledge current. Therefore, all library staff members are encouraged to pursue consortial activities.

Off-Campus Workshops/Seminars/Field Trips: It is assumed that all library staff members will find it necessary to attend off-campus workshops/ seminars/ field trips to update their job-related skills/knowledge. Therefore, all library staff members are encouraged to pursue such off-campus opportunities.

Conferences and Professional Association Activities: It is assumed that all library staff members will find it beneficial to attend at least one (some more than one) annual professional association conference and/or related activity per year. Those who are not affiliated with any professional associations are encouraged to participate in ALAO (Academic Library Association of Ohio), an association that has interest groups that support all areas of library work. Many on the staff already participate in ALAO, and the Library Director has information on the association for those interested. Individuals may choose to participate on committees of professional associations as well. Such activities will be supported in the same way as consortium activities, and need to be planned for ahead of time for budgeting purposes.

On-Campus Workshops: It is assumed that all library staff members will benefit from attending workshops and other on-campus activities that will improve their job performance on both personal and job-related levels. Such activities include, but are not limited to: computer-related workshops; management, staff, time-management, stress, and related general employee well-being workshops; and interest group meetings (hourly staff, GLCA, etc.).

Internal Library Workshops: It is assumed that all library staff members have obtained skills/knowledge in their positions or come to their positions with skills/knowledge that may, at some point, be useful to share with others on the staff. Therefore, individual staff members are encouraged to offer occasional training sessions to others on the staff on any topic or area where their expertise will assist others with their job performance. If an individual needs assistance planning such a workshop, s/he is encouraged to solicit assistance from others on the staff to do so.

Some individuals may choose to bring in outside vendors, speakers, etc. to give a workshop that is relevant to others on the staff. If this is done, expenses incurred will be charged to the library's *Travel & Entertainment* budget line. Any such workshops must be done with prior knowledge and consent of the library director. If an individual needs assistance planning such a workshop, s/he is encouraged to solicit assistance from others on the staff to do so.

Drew University Library

POLICY ON PROFESSIONAL MEETINGS, TRAVEL, AND REIMBURSEMENT FOR LIBRARY FACULTY

INTRODUCTION

The involvement of Drew's library faculty in professional organizations and other activities is an integral and important part of our professional life. The library supports such activity by providing released time and nominal financial support. Released time for attendance at meetings is a privilege, the granting of which is rarely questioned. Financial support, unfortunately, is less available.

Rather than create a hierarchy of professional activities, the library faculty asserts the principle that it is important that we each contribute to the profession as our specific library positions and personal interests incline, thereby enriching our service to Drew University. For Drew, of course, it is important that we be represented at ATLA, but it is also important that we have librarians involved in ALA, ACRL, NJLA and other groups, state- and nation-wide, identified as professionally relevant to our library faculty, library, or university.

Every librarian should consider that a small portion of the travel budget exists to support his/her professional travel costs, although our levels of activity and related costs vary. The Committee on Faculty will provide guidance to the library administration in determining what professional priorities to support among the various options available to the faculty in a given period.

The following guidelines, developed and approved by the library faculty in 1979, and slightly amended in 1983, remain essentially valid. As costs and inflation have risen, however, the size of the travel budget has remained unchanged. Hence the suggested figures cannot always be met, some of the guidelines are more ideal than real, and the administration of the budget is necessarily flexible.

POLICY

Attendance at and participation in professional and scholarly meetings and seminars is an appropriate use of part of library faculty member's time and effort. To encourage this activity, the library will support library faculty participation in professional associations by providing released time and some monetary reimbursement as budget and guidelines permit.

Every member of the library faculty is eligible to apply for a travel allotment to help finance his or her attendance at professional meetings.

Drew University Library
Madison, New Jersey

The travel budget will be administered by the library administration with the advice of the Library Committee on Faculty.

Each faculty member is eligible for one travel grant during the fiscal year (July 1 - June 30). A second grant may be considered when the faculty member is included on the official program of the meeting as an officer, speaker or committee member and funds are available.

PROFESSIONAL MEETINGS, ETC.

Faculty members should be members of the organization whose meeting they plan to attend or the program should be one that is relevant to the needs of the library.

Faculty members who receive support should file a brief report of their meeting responsibilities with the Library Committee on Faculty.

When funds are available, the following expenses will be covered in priority order:
1. Registration
2. Travel
3. Meals and lodging

For those faculty members with no official connection to the meeting, other than personal membership, registration may be paid for one meeting a year. If additional funds are available at the end of the fiscal year, their travel may be supported, fully or partially as funds permit. This may be a smaller percentage than the amount given to faculty who serve the organization in some official capacity.

When faculty members have officer, committee or speaker responsibilities, their registration fees and at least some travel expenses will be covered for one meeting a year. If additional funds are available at the end of the fiscal year, the remainder of their expenses will also be supported, fully or partially, as funds permit, or registration and travel expenses for a second meeting will be supported partially.

In addition to the above policies, local meetings may be fully reimbursed for each faculty member who submits a record of expenses. It may be that a sum is expended over a period of months in transportation costs or as a one time registration fee for a seminar in the area. Each library faculty member may apply for this type of reimbursement as often as necessary. The number of requests filled will vary. The relationship of the program attended to the needs of the library as well as to the volume of requests and the total pattern of professional involvement of the faculty members will be considered.

Drew University Library
Madison, New Jersey

PROCEDURES

Applications for grants should be made to the Director as far in advance as possible sos that the needs of the entire faculty can be seen and a preliminary level of support figure can be given to each faculty member. By October 1st of each year, faculty members should indicate in writing to the Library Committee on Faculty the meetings they plan to attend that year and list their responsibilities and estimated expenses.

Upon return from a meeting, faculty members should submit a record of their expenses to the Directory on the university voucher form with appropriate receipts attached. Reimbursement of registration fees and, where applicable, travel and expenses will follow as soon as possible. Advances for June meetings should be requested in April.

DREW UNIVERSITY LIBRARY
SABBATICALS FOR LIBRARIANS: PROCEDURES AND POLICIES

The University Faculty Personnel Policy (UFPP) of 1979 contains the basic policy regarding sabbaticals. Specific applications for librarians follow.

The University Faculty Personnel Policy specifies: "Sabbatical leave shall be for one year at half salary or for one semester at full salary." For library faculty the equivalent periods are 5 1/2 months at full salary or 11 months at half salary. Normally sabbatical leaves correspond to the semester schedule. Personal needs, sabbatical objective, and/or library needs may require an alternative model for a given request.

Vacation accrues in its regular manner. Vacation may or may not be part of the sabbatical leave, but the initial request should indicate the preference.

At present it appears that the library cannot sustain more than three sabbatical leaves in one year or more than 1.5 librarians on leave during any one semester. If more requests come to the Library Committee on Faculty, the committee will follow the guidelines in Review of Sabbatical Request by the Library Committee on Faculty (November 4, 1985).

Requests should come to the Library Committee on Faculty by October 1 of the year prior to the year requested. Normally this will be an application in the sixth year of service of the sixth year since the last sabbatical, for a leave in the seventh year.

All librarians interested in applying for a sabbatical should present a brief (two page) proposal to the committee by Oct. 1 of the year preceding the proposed sabbatical year. The proposal should address the following topics.

I. Describe your proposed project
   A. Statement of the project
   B. Purpose or goals
   C. Methodology (where, when, what, how, etc.)
   D. Probable impact (contributions to your professional development, benefits to Drew Library or Drew University, etc.)
   E. Strategy for evaluation
   F. Funding possibilities

II. Indicate the timing, duration, and vacation plans of your requested leave

III. Suggest how major aspects of your job responsibilities can be met in our absence

While there is no desire to define what type of "intensive study and research" (UFPP p. 25) is appropriate for a given sabbatical, there is a sense in the committee that all projects and proposals must offer a well-reasoned argument within the range of library and/or University goals and objectives.

After returning from sabbatical one is expected to submit an evaluative report about one's sabbatical work to the committee by the next Dec. 1.

SABBATICALS FOR LIBRARIANS

Librarians on sabbatical have the right to participate in library governance but there is no expectation that persons on sabbatical must attend meetings. A person on sabbatical should provide the library office with their preferred mailing address so that correspondence can be forwarded on a regular basis. Librarians on sabbatical will be relieved of committee responsibilities while on sabbatical at their request, but will be considered for committee appointments which would begin after their return. (See also COMMITTEES, Library Committee on Faculty, rev. July '86 for membership on LCOF while on sabbatical.)

Normally the library cannot provide funding or support services for travel, research, or clerical assistance. Limited support, however, may be available for preparation of manuscripts for publication. (See POLICY FOR DISTRIBUTION OF LIBRARY FACULTY FUNDS FOR SCHOLARLY PROJECTS, Nov. 4, 1985)

Library patron privileges continue.

All changes in approved sabbatical scheduling must be reviewed and approved once again by the Library faculty.

DREW UNIVERSITY LIBRARY

POLICY FOR DISTRIBUTION OF LIBRARY FACULTY FUNDS FOR SCHOLARLY PROJECTS

Purpose: The library will make limited funds available for support of scholarly projects, particularly those leading to publication. Applicants must be librarians with clearly defined projects in an area of academic interest. Funds may be used for expenses such as the following:

> typing of manuscripts
> photocopying of materials not readily accessible
> travel to libraries and research collections
> student research assistants
> copyright fees
> software specifically tailored to a research project
> supplementing matching grants

Amount: Librarians may apply between July and May of the fiscal year in advance of anticipated expenses up to a request of $100, and may apply for additional funding until June 15 for expenses incurred. Normally no librarian will be granted more than $300 per year. If the budget has been exhausted for the year, librarians may make requests in the following year for expenses incurred. It is the responsibility of the Library Committee on Faculty to notify librarians of available funds in the current and projected budgets in May of each year.

Procedure: Requests should be made to the Library Committee on Faculty, and allocations will be made by the Director in consultation with the Committee. Requests should contain a description of the project, plans for publication, a detailed list of projected expenses, and receipts or other documentation for actual expenses. Librarians who have received advance funding should submit a documented account of expenses for which the grant was used. Applications for funding of multi-year projects must be submitted each year.

Profits: Should a librarian gain financially from the project, funds provided by the Library should be returned.

Approved by the Library Faculty, November 4, 1985

Drew University Library

Library Faculty Personnel Policy Interpretation

VACATION

Library faculty, as exempt employees on 12 month contracts (or 11 month and vacation) earn 1.66 days of vacation a month, or 20 days in one year. 1.66 days X 7 hour days (11.62 hours) can be accumulated until one reaches a maximum of 210 hours or 30 days.

If you reach 210 hours and have taken no vacation, you will not earn anymore until you take time off. When you take a vacation day, you will have used seven hours and can then begin accumulating another seven hours vacation time.

Report all vacation time to the Personnel Office on the standard monthly vacation/sick cards.

LIBRARY FACULTY TIME

In addition to vacation, librarians as 12 month faculty are eligible to take 10 days a year to work on research projects or professional activities.

MEETING TIME

When a librarian attends a professional meeting, both he time at the meeting and reasonable travel time to and from the meeting shall be considered part of a regular work schedule.

For insurance purposes, one should tell the administrative office (in writing) when one will be away from Drew on Drew business. Reporting forms are available in the Administrative Office.

HOLIDAYS

University holidays, as listed by the University Human Resources Office, may vary from year to year. If on a given holiday, it is necessary to be at work in order to meet the needs of the faculty and students for library services, another day off should be substituted for the holiday. For example, some faculty may need to be here to join teaching faculty in giving orientation sessions on Labor Day and will need to take another day as a holiday.

RELIGIOUS HOLIDAYS

If a faculty member wishes to observe a religious holiday that is not part of the University holiday schedule, they should use one of their vacation days to do so, or substitute one of the University holidays (i.e. Good Friday for Yom Kippur. Yom Kippur is currently a day when there are no classes, but it is not a University holiday.)

SICK TIME

For university insurance purposes, Library faculty should report sick days directly to the Human Resources Office as soon as possible if they are absent for longer than five continuous working days and are under a doctor's care.

Ina Dillard Russell Library
Georgia College
Milledgeville, Georgia

GEORGIA COLLEGE LIBRARIES

TRAVEL AND STAFF* DEVELOPMENT POLICIES

Policy

The purpose of the library/media staff development program is to provide opportunities, supplementary to on-the-job training, which will enable the individual to better perform the duties of his/her position, will enhance the individual's understanding and appreciation of the library/media center and their functions, and will provide for the growth and development of the individual as a member of the library/media staff.

Staff development is a high priority for the Georgia College Library and Media Center. Goal 3, Objective 4 of the Five Year Plan of the Georgia College Libraries is "to continue to enhance each [staff] member's knowledge base via staff development workshops and/or attendance at state and regional library meetings." Staff development is regarded as a joint responsibility between the staff member and the Libraries. Individual staff are expected to take responsibility for their own growth in knowledge and skill, identifying courses, workshops, conferences and other educational, professional, or skills oriented opportunities to improve their capacity to do excellent work on behalf of the College.

Library and Media personnel may request funding and/or release time to attend meetings and conferences of local, state, and regional, or national library organizations, vendor workshops or meetings, special assemblies, workshops, seminars, institutes, committee meetings, and other formally structured discussions of professional associations. Greater encouragement is given to participation at the state and regional level.

The Georgia College Libraries encourages staff membership and participation in professional development activities by assisting staff attendance at such events as are outlined below.

*Staff - all employed personnel in the Georgia College Library or Media Center

I. Types of Travel/Professional Leave.
Staff development/travel funds for the Library and Media Center are allocated in two categories and each contributes to the overall mission of the Libraries.

A. Administrative Travel. Such travel is done at the request of the Library Administration to help the Library/Media Center accomplish its mission. Generally the staff member is the official representative of the Libraries and has the authority to speak for the Libraries in that context. Examples include, but are not limited to, SOLINET membership meetings, Regents Academic Committee meetings, collection development trips, on-site location work for production in progress, library site visits, etc. The Director of Libraries shall designate such status. Administrative travel is fully supported with released time. Reimbursement is based on availability of funds, but administrative travel is generally fully funded.

B. Professional Development and Elective Travel.
Professional development activities are self-selected and promote professional growth and knowledge and broaden perspective by providing an opportunity to meet and exchange information with staff from other similar organizations. Such activities provide staff the opportunity to bring back information to their areas on topics of concern, to keep current in their field and to make contributions to their chosen profession.

1. Travel to Conferences and Meetings. Travel funds are available to attend conferences, meetings, etc. which relate to one's work in the library/media center. Reimbursement is based on several factors such as the individual's level of responsibility in the library/media center, the relationship of the conference to the individual's work, and the number of individuals representing the Libraries at the conference. The following are recognized as professional development activities which may be fully or partially reimbursable:
   -scheduled appearance on the program of a professional association, eg, delivery of a paper, participation in panel discussion, workshop leader, etc.;
   -participation as a current officer of a professional association;
   -participation as a current officer of a committee of a professional association;
   -participation as a current committee member of a professional association;
   -attendance at a professional association in which a staff member holds membership.

Professional travel is encouraged and will be supported with released time and with reimbursement for expenses within the limits of available funds.

Ina Dillard Russell Library
Georgia College
Milledgeville, Georgia

2. Staff Education, workshops, and institutes. Two kinds of educational development are available to library/media staff members: in-house and external. 1) In-house/on-campus activities are available to all staff. The Library/Media Staff Development Committee surveys the staff, develops plans for annual development activities, and plans at least one activity per quarter (academic year) or one big event for the year for all staff. Staff may also audit or take classes for credit either on or off campus. Continuing education classes may be pertinent and helpful. Classes sponsored by other organizations and institutions are sometimes relevant. 2) External professional development may be gained by attendance at short courses, workshops, and seminars which may be recommended by a supervisor or be self-selected, enhance one's skills, and may be professionally or personally enriching. They are not necessarily library/media specific.

Educational travel funds are often available to travel to attend workshops, seminars, or other training sessions in order to improve job-related skills and to learn more about a job related area. It is expected that the attendee will bring back to the Library/Media Center skills and knowledge that could not otherwise be obtained. Such opportunities may range from a one-day secretarial skills workshop to a one-week seminar on television/video production.

Workshops, institutes, and other staff development activities are encouraged and will be fully supported with released time and with reimbursement for expenses within the limits of available funds. Reimbursement is based on several factors such as the individual's level of responsibility in the library/media center, the relationship of the conference to the individual's work, and the number of individuals representing the Libraries at the activity.

Listed below are the primary criteria to be used in determining programs which qualify for granting of released time and/or partial or full payment of expenses. These are intended as guidelines and exceptions can be made. The criteria are:
> -the program (seminar, workshop, conference, etc.) must be related to the staff member's functions and responsibilities within the library/media center.
> -the program should take place in Georgia, a bordering state, or the closest place where offered.
> -attendance must be approved by the area Coordinator and Director of Libraries.

Ina Dillard Russell Library
Georgia College
Milledgeville, Georgia

II. Funding Policy

Funding for travel will be based on availability of funds for any given year. Staff requests for travel amy be honored in one or several ways. Released time may be given, registration may be paid, partial travel may be paid, or full funding may be allocated. The library/media travel budget is sufficient for partial funding of many activities and full funding for some activities. In addition to the Libraries travel budget, funding is available from the School of Education Level I funds, College Level II Faculty Develolpment Funds, and COPE.

Oberlin College Library
Oberlin, Ohio
GUIDELINES FOR RECEIVING STAFF DEVELOPMENT FUNDS FOR TRAVEL

Oberlin College Library staff members are encouraged to join professional organizations, to attend their meetings, and to take part in programs of continuing education. The library budget includes a fund to help defray the expenses of a staff member attending such meetings and programs. In general, staff development monies are not available to fund continuing, ongoing coursework for a degree. The staff member is expected to report to the appropriate interested persons or committees about the content of the meeting or program attended.

The Staff Development Committee supervises the distribution of staff development funds. The Committee consists of three members elected from the Professional Staff and one member elected from the Administrative Assistants. Each member serves for two academic years. Two members are elected each year at the elections meeting of Library Council. The Administrative Assistants shall be polled prior to the meeting to ascertain who is willing to serve.

A goal of the Committee is to provide substantial reimbursement for one major meeting for each interested staff member. All staff members, including those with limited term appointments, are eligible for staff development funds. Staff members about to terminate their employment with the library are urged to use discretion in requesting staff development funds. It should be recognized that time granted to attend meetings without loss of pay or vacation time, while customary, is to a degree underwriting the expense of attendance. The Committee allocates funds on a first come-first served basis, and makes no attempt to judge the value of a program selected by a staff member. Since funds are limited, however, it may not always be possible to grant funding for a staff member to attend the meeting of his/her choice. The Committee is responsible for making the current status of its budget known so that, whenever possible, staff members travel with an understanding of the availability of funding.

To obtain funding, a staff member will first clear with his/her department head that time is available. S/he shall then submit a request to the chair of the Staff Development Committee, using the form APPLICATION FOR STAFF DEVELOPMENT FUNDS (rev. 10/85) available from any committee member. The form should be submitted whether or not the staff member needs an advance, so that the Committee can keep track of upcoming expenses. It should be submitted at least two weeks in advance if the staff member wishes to receive an advance.

After the travel is completed, the staff member shall submit his/her expenses on an EXPENSE REPORT FOR STAFF TRAVEL (rev. 10/85) form. All receipts shall be submitted with this form. The Committee will then authorize reimbursement by check.

The formula for allocating staff development funds will be as follows:

1. PER DIEM: $50 per night spent in a hotel up to $200 (4 days), which may be used for rooms, meals, special events and tours, etc. as the recipient wishes. When a trip involves an additional day of travel beyond the nights away, $25 will be provided, as long as the total per diem reimbursement does not exceed $200. In addition, staff members who do not pay for their lodging during their travel may collect $25 per diem.

2. TRANSPORTATION: Full reimbursement for the first $150 of transportation expenses and 1/2 of the next $300 for a maximum of $300. Transportation includes car mileage at the going college rate; bus, train, and plane fares; airport limosines; taxi fares; and parking charges. Receipts should be submitted whenever possible.

3. REGISTRATION: Up to $150 of the basic registration fees from the event. If meals or accomodations are included in the registration fee, the per diem reimbursement may be affected. For those staff members who do not spend the $50 per diem, but incur registration fees over $150, SDC will reimburse up to $50 per night away for the excess registration fee (within the limits of the existing formula).

Second trips will be funded at 1/2 the formula only after all interested staff members have been funded for their first trips. Staff members are encouraged to submit expense reports for all meetings attended so that the Committee can monitor and report on the out-of-pocket expenditures by library staff for staff development.

Committee work closely associated with one's job and local meetings (such as OCLC, NEOMAL, NOTSL, and some ALAO meetings) will usually be funded by other sources. Applications should still be channeled through the Staff Development Committee to the appropriate source.

The Committee will maintain records, monitor the funds, present periodic reports to the Library Council, and present an annual report on the distribution of funds for the year.

Approved, 6/85
Revised and approved, 12/87
Revised and approved, 3/14/90

A. L. Beeghly Library
Ohio Wesleyan University
Delaware, Ohio

M E M O R A N D U M

DATE: August, 1993. Summarized from 1990 internal staff memo.

SENT TO: Library Personnel

FROM: Kathleen List, Director of Libraries
          Reviewed and revised by the Management Team

RE: Staff Development--Release Time for Professional
          Activities

Library travel funds must cover all the training,
representative, and conference attendance expenses discussed
below, as well as other library transportation costs, including
pick up and delivery of repaired equipment, etc. The travel
budget has been apportioned accordingly. Details are not
included here, but the extent of professional activities reviewed
here will give a clearer idea of the demands on what is a
relatively small budget for a staff of 18 FTE.

Internal library guidelines on using work hours and travel
funds for professional activities or approval of unpaid time off
have been establish in lieu of more formal university guidelines
not yet available for all employee groups. Release time for
professional activities has been established at six days (45
hours) for librarians, three days (22.5 hours) for non-librarian
personnel working 975 hours or more annually, and one and one-
half days (15 hours) for those working less than 975 hours
annually.

Review
In order to determine how much paid release time is
appropriate for professional activities not directly encompassing
a staff member's job responsibilities, the management team
reviewed the kinds and amount of paid leave already in place.
The dollar value of the time a library staff member might
typically be out of the building for paid leave activities of all
kinds, including the three-day equivalent (22.5 hours) release
time guidelines for professional activities, is twenty-five
percent of that person's annual salary.

Taken into account the recent adjustments in our internal
personnel practices which now recognize compensatory time due
staff members for participation in required library activities
outside normal office hours, such as the two-night student
assistant orientation, LS/2000 backup responsibilities, and
working on Labor Day.

Job-Related or Benefits-Related Activities
Further discussion here of paid professional release time
assumes the following activities are already recognized as within
a staff member's job responsibilities or university benefits
package. Thus, the following are not charged against
professional release time.

(1) Workshops or meetings attended at the direction of the supervisor to add or upgrade skills and information needed in the job. Example: Advanced training on ACQ350; attendance at an informational meeting on the upcoming changes in the implementation of the OCLC PRISM software; attendance at the forthcoming CALICO discussion on Copyright.

(2) Attending meetings on behalf of the library as its appointed, elected, or recognized representative. Example: participation in the annual LS/2000 Users Group Meeting; attending OHIONET meetings as appointed representatives to the ILL and Acquisitions Advisory Councils; attendance at GODORT meetings as government depository library representative; attendance at the September CALICO meeting.

(3) Attending the GLCA Staff Network meeting.

(4) Taking one OWU undergraduate course per semester.

(5) Participation in library programs or meetings sponsored by and presented on the OWU campus. Example: OLA Central Ohio Chapter Annual Conference held in Beeghly Library

Exceptional Activities Requiring Review and Approval

Also excluded are the providing of workshops, training, or services during normally scheduled office hours but outside one's normal job responsibilities. Whether or not an additional stipend is received, prior approval of the Director of Libraries is required--and sometimes the Director of Human Resources-- before compensatory time, unpaid leave, or vacation time may be scheduled for these activities. Example: leading Wordperfect workshops funded by the Academic Dean's office; presenting workshops for church library managers.

Professional Release Time

Activities charged against paid professional release time include the following: (Note: Inclusion of an activity here does not imply that travel funds will automatically be available or approved to support that activity.)

(1) Attendance at meetings or conferences of local, regional, or national professional organizations or service to those organizations. Example: ALAO, ALA, ACRL, OLA, MAC as an officer, organizer, or participant.

Occasionally, exceptional service to an office in one organization may be cause for granting additional release time for a specified period of time. Staff members should be prepared to use personal time or other paid leave such as vacation, optional holiday, or accrued compensatory time when making commitments to multiple responsibilities in professional organizations.

(2) Undergraduate, licensing, or certificate programs in library-related subjects taken at institutions other than OWU

(3) Programs of study leading to advanced degrees in library-related subjects.

(4) Other related continuing education opportunities. Example: attendance at a conference on hypermedia for computer-assisted instruction.

Ripon College Library
Ripon, Wisconsin

Ripon College Library
Professional Development Policy
Revised
March 22, 1989

Purpose: This policy is written in an effort to promote, stimulate and coordinate professional activities among the librarians.

Policy: Each librarian is responsible for active participation in teaching, research and service. Teaching in the context of the library refers to those duties and activities necessary to carry out the function of one's appointed position and necessary to the library's operation and participation in the academic community. These teaching responsibilities are considered assigned time and comprise not less than 80 percent of the work week. They include, first and foremost, the functions of one's position and they incorporate service in the form of time spent in professional meetings directly relating to library operations and college committee work.

Research, generally leading to publication, and professional development, including meetings contributing to general professional growth, are considered part of the librarian's activities and comprise not more than 20 percent of the work week. It is recognized however, that this amount of time will not be sufficient to complete all such activities and responsibilities, which implies the need to supplement unassigned time with the use of one's personal time. Since the number of librarians at Ripon College is so small and service to students and faculty is foremost, it may not be possible for all of the librarians to engage in research during any one term. If all librarians have immediate research needs during a particular term, then all will have to relinquish some of their research time in order to provide adequate library service. Ultimately, the library director has the discretion to permit or restrict research time.

Implementation: Unassigned time should be determined in accord with and relative to needs dictated by research and other professional development activities in which the librarian is engaged. There needs to be agreement between the librarian and the library director on the scheduling of unassigned time to ensure adequate coverage of the library during peak user periods. In August and January of each year, the librarians will meet to establish their research schedules for the forthcoming term.

The librarian should provide the director with informal short reports of his/her use of unassigned time throughout the year and in summary to be added to the library director's annual report.

Approved by the librarians: March 22, 1989
Approved by the Dean: April 10, 1989

Alcuin Library
Saint John's University/College of Saint Benedict
Collegeville, Minnesota

Staff Development Policy

Staff Development activities (as covered by the appropriate personnel handbook) include:

1. Sabbatical/long term leave.

2. SJU/CSB classes/courses

3. Conferences/conventions/workshops, etc.

This policy applies to all library, media, and computer staff.

A distinction is made between these activities that are specifically related to job function (i.e. it is requested that the employee take specific training, or the employee and supervisor agree is work-related) to be referred to as training, and those activities that an individual wishes to undertake that are not directly related to job function, but have long term benefits for the individual and the organization (to be referred to as staff development).

Since we operate with limited funding, work-related activities will have precedence over non-work activities.

Two committees are involved in Staff Development activities:

A standing committee (Associate Director's group) is ultimately responsible for the allocation of staff development resources.

A committee made up of representatives of each of the areas will plan and implement at least three full staff programs per year on library/media/academic computing issues. The chair of the committee will be one of the associate directors. Areas represented include: CSB library public services; SJU library public services; Media; Academic Computing; and joint library technical services. The representative of an area will serve two years and be responsible for the appointment of his or her successor to the committee at the end of that time.

All requests for funding should be requested in writing and discussed with the immediate supervisor, who will forward the proposal to the chair of the Staff Development committee to bring to the Associate Director's committee for a decision.

Requests for released time should also be submitted to this group using the same process.

Alcuin Library
Saint John's University/College of Saint Benedict
Collegeville, Minnesota

The three defined categories of activities:

1. Sabbatical / long-term leave.

Decisions on sabbaticals/long term leave are left to the discretion of the individual requesting the leave, the supervisor, and the Director. Decisions on these activities involve long range planning.

2. Classes / courses (CSB/SJU)

An individual may take one course per Spring or Fall semester.
Time must be made up.

(NB Exceptions may be made to the rule regarding make-up time in exceptional cases at the Director's discretion; ie in cases essential skills are needed.)

3. Conferences/ conventions/ workshops

Work related activities take precedence over all other activities.

Individuals presenting papers deserve institutional support. Other funding avenues outside the library budgets will be investigated for these occasions. If such funding is not available, work-related presentations will receive highest priority in this category.

Individuals with State of the Art, more immediate information needs, take precedence over long-term informational or educational opportunities.

Support Staff development needs will be of high priority.

Depending upon the availability of funds, if it is requested that the employee attend a particular workshop/conference etc for work-related reasons, the following expenses shall be reimbursed:

a. Travel expenses (parking, mileage, airfare, etc.)
b. Reasonable room and per diem
c. Fees

For all other activities, reimbursement for any or all of the above depends upon the availability of funds.

7/5/91 amended

Widener University

WOLFGRAM MEMORIAL LIBRARY
Office of the Director

The Pennsylvania Campus
Chester, Pennsylvania 19013
(215) 499-4086, 4087
Fax (215) 499-4588

LIBRARIAN'S STAFF DEVELOPMENT FUND

Mr. Lee C. Brown, former Director of the Wolfgram Library, established an endowment fund at the time of his retirement for the future use and benefit of any or all staff members.

The purpose is "to assist in developing, enhancing and updating the technical and professional knowledge and skills of the Wolfgram Memorial Library staff members."

The endowment's earned income is to be spent under the guidance of the "Fund Trustees" consisting of "the Head Librarian, the Librarian Emeritus, the Assistant Librarian and one at-large Trustee elected by and from the staff".

The Trustees agreed that the funds should be used in addition to and not in lieu of budgeted library funds currently available for staff training.

1. Recipients should be those who can identify an educational program, course, professional exchange opportunity, research project, etc., primarily to enhance their own personal professional growth. The current need of our library is a secondary qualification for the award. All staff members who need some financial support to meet their individual career goals are eligible to apply.
Examples for projects receiving an award would be:
a. Tuition or fee for a specific course, summer school, management training institute, etc.
b. Stipend to help replace salary for someone taking leave of absence without pay while undertaking an educational or research project.
c. Travel and living expenses during a study or research project, or to facilitate an exchange arrangement, etc.

The proposal should include a complete description of the project including its cost and time period, and the goal and benefit for the applicant. Documentation to explain its scope may be attached. It is assumed that the applicant will contribute personal funds as well, and publish or share the results with library colleagues in some manner.

Training sessions directly related to one's job and its current and future responsibilities, (e.g. PALINET workshops) will continue to be funded through the library budget.

Individual requests for these special funds are to be submitted using the attached form. The "Trustees" will review and select the recipients based on merit of the proposal and of the applicant, and within the limits of currently available funds. Those who wish to apply and need more guidance in planning their project should turn to the Library Director or Assistant Director for assistance.

Wolfgram Memorial Library
Widener University
Chester, Pennsylvania

2. In addition to individual awards, these funds can be used to bring expert speakers or workshop moderators to our library to deal with issues of general interest to all staff members. We will be preparing a survey asking all of you to indicate your interests in order to plan such in-house seminars.

Information on current workshops, career development opportunities, etc. have been and will be circulated to all staff, inserted in the Information File, etc. Reading material there may suggest some topics of value to us here and now.

We are fortunate to have these special funds. The success of its projects, the benefits to you will depend greatly on your input and interest.

11/17/87

WOLFGRAM MEMORIAL LIBRARY

Librarian's Fund for Staff Development

Application form to request special funds for individual educational, research or other career development projects. To be submitted to the Library Director for review by the Trustees. Applications may be submitted twice a year, not later than January 31 or May 31. The Trustees will make their selection within one month. You may be interviewed by the committee before final decision to grant award.

Name of applicant _____

    Date of Application _____

    Library Position _____

Proposed project to be funded:

    Name, description _____

            (attach pertinent documentation

    Duration (dates) _____

    Location _____

    Type of project (check which applies)

            higher education course for credit _____

            professional workshop _____

            independent research _____

            job exchange _____

            writing for publication _____

            free consultant service _____

            Other _____

            _____

            _____

            _____

Proposed budget ($ amounts)

            cost of program (fee/tuition)   _____

            living expenses   _____

            travel expenses   _____

            other (specify)   _____

            projected salary loss   _____

            scholarship or award received   _____

Librarian's Staff Development Fund - 51

personal contribution   _____
other financial considerations
describe _____

What do you expect to gain from this project for you personal career?

_____

_____

_____

In what form will you share the results?
  written report inhouse _____
  publication _____
      Name _____
  teaching material _____
      (e.g. syllabus, manual, video, computer program, etc.)
  other _____

_____
Signature

11/24/87

College-wide Staff Development Policies

These colleges indicated that they followed college-wide staff development policies rather than policies written specifically by/for the library.

2.11 Faculty Development

2.11.1 Sabbatical Leave

Faculty policy on Sabbatical Leaves is found in Section 2.8.3.

2.11.2 Professional Meeting Allowance

The College allows $500 per year to each full-time member of the teaching faculty toward expenses incurred in attending meetings of professional associations. An adjunct faculty member is allowed an amount proportionate to his/her teaching load. This allowance may be accumulated for up to two years, for a total of no more than $1000. The Dean of the College should be consulted regarding this allowance.

2.11.3 Supplemental Professional Meeting Allowance

The Faculty Development Fund includes money intended to supplement the faculty professional meeting allowance, thereby permitting and encouraging increased faculty participation at conferences, workshops, institutes, and faculty internships.

To apply for funds, faculty members should submit a request to the Dean's Office. Requests can be submitted during any term, regardless of when one plans to travel during the year. Since the monies will be allocated on request, and thus will not necessarily be distributed equally throughout the year, it is in the best interest of the individual to apply for funding as early as possible. The deadline for requests is the second Friday of each term. To qualify for these funds, individuals must provide evidence that their regular professional meeting allowance has been spent or committed for the current academic year.

Applications will be rank ordered according to the following priorities: (a) first preference will be given to individuals delivering papers, chairing sessions, or serving as discussants at conferences; (b) second priority is accorded faculty members attending conferences, institutes, workshops, or faculty internships that have direct relevance to specific courses they teach; and (c) depending on the availability of funds, all other requests to attend conferences, institutes, workshops, or faculty internships will then be considered.

Faculty members may not submit more than one request per term. While in general $500 should be considered the maximum amount available per year, in rare exceptions, at the discretion of the Dean, that amount may be exceeded.

2.11.4   Research and Sabbatical Leave Grants

A.   Purpose of these Grants

The Research and Sabbatical Leave grants are designed to contribute to the teaching program of the College by promoting faculty excellence. The grants are to enable faculty members to develop as scholars and teachers by making possible sustained and significant academic endeavors.

The grants may be used to support research, creative work, or additional study but are not intended for the completion of terminal degree requirements.

B.   Nature of the Grants

Four grants may be awarded annually for work to be completed during the following summer or academic year:

(1) two sabbatical stipends of $3,600 each
(2) two research stipends of $1,800 each

The award would not preclude accepting other sources of financial assistance such as sabbatical support, fellowships, or foundation grants.

C.   Eligibility

All full-time faculty members who are eligible for a sabbatical are eligible for a $3,600 grant. This grant will be made only in conjunction with a sabbatical of two or three terms. Sabbatical proposals must have prior approval through normal channels.

All non-tenured faculty members who have taught at least one full year at Augustana are eligible to apply for an $1,800 grant.

2

D. <u>Guidelines and Selection</u>

The award of these grants will be made by the Augustana
Research Foundation upon recommendation of the Faculty
Research Committee.

Guidelines for application and selection are the same as those
used for the Augustana Faculty Research Fund awards. (See
Section 2.11.5)

E. <u>Presentations by Grantees</u>

Each grantee will be expected to give a lecture or other
presentation during the academic year following his or her
grant. The presentations will be publicized events to which
the public will be invited.

3

Career Development Planning

Approved: 6/86	*Replaces: IIB.4-IIb.42b*
Revised: 9.15/89	

The Career Development Program is an effort to foster the professional development of the faculty in ways benefiting both the individual and the college. It is designed to capitalize on the mutual interest of the college and its faculty in the intellectual vitality and continuing personal development of those on whose competence the future of the educational programs of the college most depends.

The purpose of the Career Development Plan is to provide a context for reviewing all major considerations of faculty personnel -- tenure, promotion, sabbaticals and unpaid leaves, and periodic evaluations -- as well as requests for Career Development Implementation Grants. These plans differ from each other as do the roles of the faculty within the college and within the academic profession. Common to all such plans are the faculty member's statements of background and present situation, short-term and long-range goals for professional development, plans for formative evaluation, and perspectives on summative evaluation.

The preparation of the Career Development Plan is the responsibility of the faculty member. The individual normally prepares a draft with the advice of a career development advisor and submits the plan to the relevant department chair(s) and program director(s) and finally to the division dean for review and comment. When satisfied that the completed plan provides an appropriate and adequate context within which the mutual interests of the college and the individual may be pursued, the dean, on behalf of the Faculty Review and Promotion Committee, gives the individual a letter or memorandum of acceptance and places the Career Development Plan in the faculty personnel file. Where substantial differences of interpretation arise, the faculty member may appeal to the vice president for academic affairs.

New faculty normally complete a Career Development Plan in their second year at the college. A tenure track member of the faculty will carefully review and revise this plan and submit it to the relevant department chair(s) and finally to the division dean for acceptance no later than September 1 of the academic year of tenure consideration. Career Development Plans are subsequently revised every five or six years. As circumstances or goals change, individuals may prepare through the same process briefer supplements to the current plan.

The Faculty Review and Promotion Committee will make no positive recommendation concerning tenure, promotion, or sabbatical without first reviewing an accepted and current Career Development Plan. Normally, Career Development Implementation Grants will be awarded only for purposes within the scope of a current plan, through exceptions may be made for faculty whose original Career Development Plans are not yet due for completion.

Section: Personnel Policies and Procedures -- Faculty

Abell Library
Austin College
Sherman, Texas

Subject: **Career and Professional Development for Faculty**

Page 2 of 3

Role of Career Development Advisors

The president after consultation with the vice president for academic affairs and the division deans shall appoint members of the faculty to serve as career development advisors, normally for terms of four years.

Career development advisors respond to faculty requests for advice and information. At the faculty member's initiative, a career development advisor may provide 1) information about the Career Development Program, 2) assistance in planning formative evaluation, 3) advice concerning improvement of teaching, and 4) consultation and editorial assistance in writing a Career Development Plan or proposal.

It is not the responsibility of a career development advisor to act as an advocate or to monitor the professional development of those who seek advice or to remediate weaknesses in their teaching, nor does the advisor prepare faculty members for summative evaluation.

Membership in Professional and Learned Societies

| Approved: 8/81 | Replaces: IIB.36 |
| Revised: 9.15/89 | |

The college encourages faculty to hold membership and participate in the activities of professional and learned societies. Travel expenses for attendance at professional meetings are reimbursed to the extent allowed by the division budgets for faculty professional travel, and in accordance with college policies and division priorities. The college bears the cost of institutional membership in selected professional and learned societies but does not bear the cost of individual memberships.

In addition to division budgets for faculty professional travel, there are other sources of funding for faculty and staff travel, each having its distinctive purposes and administrative controls. These are described under "Funds for Professional Development" in this policy.

Funding for Professional Development

| Approved: 8/81 | Replaces: IIB.361 |
| Revised: 9.15/89 | |

Funds for professional development activities --including travel to professional meetings, research, course development, program revision, sabbatical support, etc. -- are available from six different sources. These funding sources and the guidelines for allocation of funds are listed below.

1. *Faculty Professional Travel Budgets* -- The purpose of these funds is to support faculty participation in professional societies, for the maintenance and development of professional status. The funds are allocated by division deans from regular division budgets.

2. *Program Development Funds (Cullen Fund)* -- Cullen funds are intended to support faculty and staff travel and other expenses in workshops and other events, for the development of

 Operational Guide

Austin College programs. Cullen funds are allocated by the authority of the Academic Affairs Committee.

3. *Career Development Funds (Richardson Fund)* -- Richardson funds are intended to support faculty and staff travel and other expenses in accordance with a college-approved Career Development Plan. Richardson funds are allocated by authority of the Academic Affairs Committee for faculty and by the Staff Benefits Committee for staff, with detailed management in the office of the vice president for academic affairs.

4. *Continuing or Recurrent Special Funds* -- These funds are allocated primarily from restricted endowments and special programs and are designated primarily for enhancement of campus programs rather than for travel. The funds are allocated by designated authority in accordance with the purposes and policies of the particular fund.

5. *Department and Division Budgets* -- Funds are available when faculty and staff are asked to travel to represent the college with one or more of its external constituencies or to carry out programs of the college. The funds are allocated by department chairs or division deans according to approved policies.

6. *Non-College Funds* -- Examples include funds for NEH Seminars, travel subsidies for principal officers as provided by some professional societies, and funds from the individual's own resources. If college funds are not involved, the college usually does not control allocation of the funds.

General Guidelines for Travel

See OP 5, "Travel and Use of Vehicles," in the "General Operational Policies and Procedures" section of this guide.

Approved: 8/81	*Replaces: IIB.362*
Revised: 9.15/89	

Education Benefits

Educational benefits are available to full-time
faculty and "regular" staff employees (see
"Definitions," PP 2) who complete nine

Approved:	9.15/89	Replaces: IIA.28, IIA.281,
Revised:	9.18/91	IIA.282, IIA.283

months of full-time employment. All eligibility ends on the date the employee ceases to be a
"regular" employee or faculty member. In case of an employee's death or disability, the
dependent's eligibility terminates at the end of the academic year; in the case of resignation or
termination, eligibility terminates at the end of the current academic term.

Qualified Tuition Reduction -- All Employees

Regular employees (staff and faculty) and their qualified dependents are eligible for certain
benefits after nine months' employment. The schedule of benefits is available from the
Personnel Office. All or part of the waiting period is waived if an employee was eligible for
tuition benefits at a previous place of employment. Assistance is limited to "tuition" only.
Applicants must meet the regular admission requirements and will be admitted to classes on a
"space available" basis unless an employee is seeking a degree and has an approved degree plan,
in which case an employee would be eligible for classes as other regular students. Exclusions
include room, board, fees, courses of private instruction, continuing education courses, special
costs for a January term field trip, any off-campus expenditure, TAGER course charges, or other
non-tuition costs.

Enrollment in Austin College courses by employees needs to be reviewed with the Executive for
the Division for the purpose of coordinating work assignments and other responsibilities.
Normally a full-time employee may not enroll for more than one course during their normal
work week. Employees must make up the time lost within the same week (Saturday through
Friday) in order to comply with the Fair Labor Standards Act.

Off-Campus "Non-Reciprocal" Awards

These awards are available to dependent children of regular employees. The following
limitations apply:

1. The dependent is enrolled as a full time undergraduate in a fully accredited institution.

2. Awards are for academic semesters or quarter terms and specifically exclude summer,
   January term, or equivalent terms.

3. Awards are limited to four academic years for each student (enrollment at Austin College
   with an on-campus tuition waiver is covered by this four-year provision).

 Operational Guide

4. At institutions with which Austin College does not have a tuition exchange agreement, Austin College will pay a stipend up to a maximum of $500 per semester and $1000 for a full academic year (tuition for quarter terms will be pro rated at $333 per term). The stipend is limited to tuition and required fees.

5. A dependent cannot receive an AC off-campus reciprocal or non-reciprocal award and an AC tuition award concurrently.

Awards at Cooperating Institutions

Dependent children are eligible to participate in Austin College's Tuition Exchange Program with participating institutions in the Association of Presbyterian Colleges and Universities and several other colleges and universities with which Austin College has agreements. Contact the director of admission for more information.

Career Development for Staff

Regular employees are encouraged to pursue programs of study and job skill improvement activities to increase individual competence.

| Approved: | 7.1/89 | Replaces: IIC.5 |
| Revised: | 9.15/89 | |

Qualifications

As a regular employee, employed 27.5 hours or more per week, the applicant must complete 9 months of service before expected use of career development funds.

Procedures

1. Contact the Personnel Office for an instruction sheet.

2. Complete application and submit it to the supervisor and/or executive for signature.

3. Return the application to the Personnel Office.

4. Applicants receiving funds will file a report with the Personnel Office, with a copy to the appropriate executive demonstrating career enhancement within 30 days after the use of the funds. This is a requisite for additional funding.

Other Guidelines

1. For the period July 1 through December 31, submit the application to the Personnel Office by June 1. Fifty percent of available funds are reserved for this period.

 Operational Guide

2. For the period January 1 through June 30, submit the application to the Personnel Office by December 1. Fifty percent of available funds are reserved for this period.

3. The Career Development Committee will meet periodically to consider additional requests but does not usually meet during the months of August, September, November and May.

4. Funds are appropriated on a fiscal year basis and may not be carried forward to the next fiscal year.

5. Priority will be given to a continuing plan that spans more than one year.

6. The Career Development Committee will meet during the month of an application deadline to review and award funds. The decision of the committee is final.

7. Preference will be given to requests that enhance current employment and/or anticipated opportunities within Austin College. In addition, each award will be determined, in part, by number of applicants and available funding.

8. $500 is reserved for on campus workshops to develop skills for support and administrative staff. The director of personnel will submit a proposed budget and schedule of workshops for these funds at the June meeting for the next fiscal year.

9. Any single award may not exceed $500 or 10% of the total pool, whichever is less.

10. An individual may not receive more than $1000 or 20% of the total pool, whichever is less, in a fiscal year.

11. In making the awards, consideration will first be given to the use of other funds, such as departmental funds, since Career Development Funds are not intended to replace departmental funds. Consideration will also be given first to other benefits, such as "Qualified Tuition Reduction."

Eligible Programs

1. Degree programs -- bachelor's, master's, and doctorate

    Reimbursable costs: a. tuition, up to 100%
                           b. fees, up to 100%
                           c. books, up to 75%
                           d. travel, up to 50%
                           e. room, up to 50%
                           f. food, up to $5.00 per day

 Operational Guide

Abell Library
Austin College   Personnel Policies and Procedures -- All Employees   Index: PP 19
Sherman, Texas
   Subject: **Benefits -- Education and Professional Development**   Page 4 of 4

2. Seminars, lectures or workshops to increase productivity, professional preparation, or knowledge

    Reimbursable costs: a.   fees, up to 100%
                            b.   travel, up to 50%
                            c.   food, up to $5.00 per day

3. Normally, funds for annual meetings or any conferences sponsored by professional associations--national, regional or local--will not be available.

Career Development for Faculty

Refer to policy PP 43, "Career and Professional Development for Faculty."

 Operational Guide

Training & Development Plan

FY 1992 - FY 1993

University staff training and development activities must be supportive of the
~ls and objectives of the institution. The Training and Development Plan for FY 1992-
~3 identifies goals and objectives that meet the needs of the University and the staff,
~ provide direction for the expenditure of resources.

GOAL

To improve the professional knowledge, skills, and abilities of University
~ployees, in order to better serve the students and the community.

OBJECTIVES

To develop and maintain an ongoing management training program for University
~mployees.

To expand and strengthen the orientation process for new employees of the
~niversity.

To increase awareness of training opportunities within the University and
~ommonwealth system.

To identify resources which can be utilized to support the Training and Development
~lan.

To develop and maintain an ongoing,professional development process by offering a
~ariety of courses, workshops, and seminars designed to educate and motivate
~mployees.

To evaluate training and development programs through a participant questionnaire.

To evaluate training and development programs through supervisory interviews to be
~onducted by the Training Coordinator.

Thomas Stanley Library
Ferrum College
Ferrum, Virginia

PROFESSIONAL DEVELOPMENT AT FERRUM COLLEGE

(FROM FERRUM COLLEGE FACULTY HANDBOOK)

FACULTY DEVELOPMENT FUND

Eligibility:

   Faculty members at Ferrum College (including library and coaching personnel holding faculty status) are eligible for grants for faculty development projects. The Faculty Development Fund from which the grant money is disbursed is administered by the Dean of the College; application should be made to the Dean's Office on the standard form available from that office. Deadline for application is November 1 for projects to begin January 1 - June 30; deadline is March 15 for projects to begin July 1 - December 31.

Stipulations:

A. Grants may be awarded for: (1) Projects involving scholarly research or participation in peer workshops or seminars. (2) Degree completion projects. Category 1 proposals should be funded at least equally with category 2 proposals during any given year. (Faculty-Staff Writing Workshop awards should not be totaled in with the category 1 awards in determining the annual apportionment).

B. In consideration of degree completion proposals, probability of near-term completion and overall probability of completion will be considered. There will be a limit of $3,000 total disbursement to an individual for doctoral work, $2,000 toward a master's degree.

C. Individual awards will be limited to a ceiling of 7.5 percent of the fund total for the year.

D. The grantee must agree to return to Ferrum College for one academic year of service as repayment. Otherwise, the grantee must actually pay the amount of the grant with interest.

E. Approval of a project will be based on the following criteria specified on the standard application form:

   1. Description of the scope and purpose of the project.

   2. Explanation of how the project will benefit the faculty member in developing his or her professional capabilities.

   3. Explanation of how the project will further benefit the college.

4. A resume of professional qualification for undertaking the project.

5. Inclusion of a budget of proposed expenses for the project, specifying the amount of money requested from the fund.

F. In consideration of projects of approximately equal merit, higher faculty rank or tenured status will be honored, although every effort will be made to encourage broad participation in the program.

G. The standard form for reporting on the project must be filed with the Dean's Office to verify expenses as outlined in the original application. Monies not expended will be returned to the fund. Any individual who does not file a report on a funded project will be ineligible for further funding.

H. Money for travel to conferences or meetings should not be disbursed from this fund but should be disbursed from divisional travel budgets.

CHEATHAM FELLOWSHIP PROGRAM

The Cheatham Fellowship is an annual grant award from an endowed fund intended to promote professional development among faculty at Ferrum College. The Dean of the College, in consultation with the President, will choose the recipient among the senior faculty applicants (professors and associate professors). The Cheatham Fellow must be an individual held in high regard as a teacher and be engaged in professional development activities which enhance his or her own and the college's reputations. The application, to be filed on the standard form available in the Dean's Office, should present a proposal that sets forth a clear and coherent academic purpose. A resume and other supporting documents may be attached at the applicant's discretion. Deadline for application is April 1, with the award being announced annually at Commencement.

The Cheatham Fellowship may fund a variety of the recipient's professional development activities during the year, with funds drawn from:

1. A grant to be used for study and individual professional development activities

2. A grant to cover expenses related to study and individual professional development activities (e.g. expenses for travel or research, clerical help, or equipment)

The latter grant is awarded only up to the amount actually expended for said activities. The Dean of the College will announce the exact amount available to be awarded in a given year.

FRANKLIN PIERCE COLLEGE

Rindge, New Hampshire 03461
603-899-5111

FRANKLIN PIERCE COLLEGE AND RINDGE FACULTY FEDERATION
AMERICAN FEDERATION OF TEACHERS AFL-CIO
COLLECTIVE BARGAINING AGREEMENT 1991-1994

ARTICLE TEN

FACULTY DEVELOPMENT

I.   The College and the Federation recognize the importance
     of continued development of Faculty members individually
     and collectively in order to encourage creative teaching
     and to contribute to the ongoing development of the
     College.

II. Each full-time Faculty member will have an expense
     allowance of up to $100 during each of the years of this
     agreement for professional memberships, journal
     subscriptions to professional publications, and materials
     related to teaching. Funds will be awarded only upon
     presentation to the Dean of an appropriate bill, statement,
     or other documentation for such expenses. These funds will
     be available through May 15 of each year. Unexpended funds
     will not revert to the Faculty Development Committee.

III. Furthermore, the College will establish a Faculty
     Development Fund of $12,500 during each of the years of
     this agreement. These monies may be used by individual
     Faculty members for travel, conferences, professional
     dues, subscriptions, growth contracts, tuition for under-
     graduate courses relevant to their teaching
     responsibilities, and other related activities. This Fund
     is in addition to the expense allowance described in
     Article 10:II.

     A. $2500 shall be reserved to fund travel to professional
         events where the Faculty member will present a paper,
         chair a session, or take some other active role.

     B. The Fund shall be administered by the Dean after
         consideration of recommendations from the Faculty
         Development Committee. Requests for funding shall be
         made in writing to the committee in accordance with
         procedures developed by the committee.

     C. The annual allocation for the Fund shall initially be
         divided equally between the two semesters. In the
         event the fall semester allocation is not completely
         utilized, the remaining portion shall be available for
         the spring semester and appropriate summer activities.

     D. Division Directors are not eligible to request
         monies from the fund.

68 - Faculty Development

IV.   The College shall reimburse permanent full-time Faculty
      members for tuition charges incurred for graduate level
      courses of study as provided herein. Faculty members are
      eligible to request such funding after a minimum of one
      year of full-time teaching at the College.

   A.   Each permanent full-time Faculty member in good
        standing qualifies for payment for two (2) courses
        per year except as limited below.

   B.   Any full-time Faculty member in good standing who is
        formally accepted and enrolled in a degree program in
        his or her teaching field qualifies for tuition for
        four (4) courses per year.

   C.   The College shall pay 85% of tuition charges covered by
        this Section up to a maximum of $10,000 on behalf of a
        Faculty member covered by this Agreement; beyond
        $10,000, the College will cover 75% of tuition charges
        provided that the coursework covered thereby is part of
        a formal degree program.

   D.   For each $5,000 in tuition payments made on behalf of
        a Faculty member, he or she will be expected to remain
        employed at the College for at least one additional
        year after the course has been completed.

   E.   The Dean will administer payments for graduate level
        courses in keeping with the provisions of this
        Article.

   F.   A Faculty member contemplating use of the provisions
        of this Section in an upcoming fiscal year must inform
        the Dean of this in writing no later than May 1. Such
        notice must include information regarding the
        institution to be attended, the number of courses to
        be taken, and the probable tuition per course.

   G.   The maximum budget provisions for tuition charges for
        Faculty members covered by this agreement will be
        $12,500 per year. Priority will be given to
        individuals currently enrolled in a degree program.
        Others will be funded on a first-come, first-serve
        basis.

Faculty Development - 69

14

H. Tuition payments will normally be made on a reimbursement basis contingent upon satisfactory completion of the course(s) as evidenced by presentation of a grade report and a statement of tuition charges from the graduate institution. However, the College may elect to advance funds for tuition payments if the Faculty member signs a personal note satisfactory to the College ensuring that the funds will be repaid to the College if the courses are not successfully completed. The College may also require an installment payroll deduction authorization to be signed in such circumstances.

V. Sabbatical leaves are awarded primarily for professional development purposes, not for personal reasons.

A. A Faculty member shall be eligible for sabbatical leave after completion of six years of full-time employment at the College.

B. Except as noted in Section C below, Faculty members are eligible for sabbatical leaves for each period of twelve regular semesters of teaching. Such leave may be granted for one semester at full salary or two semesters at half salary.

C. Sabbatical leave may be granted for one semester at half salary upon the Faculty member's completion of six regular semesters of teaching from the date of the completion of his/her most recent sabbatical leave.

D. Applications for sabbatical leave shall be made in appropriate form to the Faculty Affairs Committee and shall include a detailed statement of the professional development objectives to be sought during the sabbatical. The application shall be accompanied by a statement from the Division Director regarding his or her assessment of the value of the proposed sabbatical.

E. Eligibility to apply for a sabbatical does not imply that the sabbatical can be approved for the requested time frame. Factors to be considered by the Faculty Affairs Committee and the Dean shall include, but not be limited to: when the individual became eligible; the length of time since the last sabbatical; the strength of the rationale for the sabbatical; teaching needs in the applicant's discipline; sabbatical requests from colleagues in the discipline.

F. All rights and benefits under this Agreement shall continue in force during the sabbatical leave.

70 - Faculty Development

G. A Faculty member who takes a sabbatical is obligated to
    return to the College to teach for a period of time at
    least as long as the duration of the sabbatical.
    Failure to do so will result in the Faculty member's
    incurring an obligation to repay to the College an
    amount equal to the total cost of his/her compensation
    during the sabbatical.

CHAPTER IV - FACULTY DEVELOPMENT PROGRAM[*]

The College maintains a vigorous faculty development program. A Coordinator of Faculty Development, appointed annually, works with the Dean of Faculty and the Instruction Committee in administering the program.

The sub-programs described below will be funded within the limits imposed by the budget for faculty development each year as supplemented by any special funds secured.

Consulting With Individuals

As time permits, the Coordinator of Faculty Development is available to faculty members for confidential consultation about teaching, other areas of faculty responsibility, and career choices. Assistance can take a number of forms, including sitting in on classes and providing subsequent feedback, sharing of ideas and experience, referral to appropriate books and articles, and assistance in gaining access to development opportunities such as faculty exchanges.

Faculty Professional Development Grants

Grants may support (a) research or creative work, (b) course improvement, or (c) enhancement of professional capabilities. Preference will be given to work that promises to improve the quality and effectiveness of the educational program of the College in the short or long run. Grants will be modest in extent, and may usefully be used to start work that can be continued with external support. *Funding ordinarily will not be provided for faculty salaries or stipends.* The following will apply to reimbursement of tuition for formal study: :

(1) Courses must be at the post-baccalaureate level at an accredited institution and not available at Linfield; they need not be taken for a degree.

(2) When the faculty member continues to teach at Linfield while taking such courses, maximum reimbursement is limited by both credits and cost per credit: Reimbursement may be provided for a maximum of five credits in any semester or quarter in an amount per credit not to exceed the graduate tuition charged at Linfield (adjusted as necessary for a quarter system).

In contrast, when the faculty member is on leave while taking such courses, reimbursement is limited by dollars only: In this case the faculty member may be reimbursed for as many credits as can be purchased within the cost of five Linfield graduate credits. If the leave is for an entire year, the limit is the cost of 10 Linfield credits.

---

[*] See also the section on Faculty Evaluation in Chapter III and Appendix I.

In all cases, reimbursement will be made upon submission of proof of course completion with a grade of "B" or better.

(3) Proposals are to be submitted in advance of enrolling in the course(s). In addition to the other requirements below, the proposal must include the written approval of the department chairperson.

(4) Study supported by this policy must be germane to the faculty member's work at Linfield. Except as approved under the section below on "Changes in Professional Emphasis," support for post-baccalaureate study is not available for career changes.

(5) Grants will be within the constraints of the Dean's faculty development budget.

When travel support is requested, as to attend workshops or training programs, normal travel subvention policies will apply. In general, budget restrictions may require "cost-sharing" between the individual and the College.

Proposals in any category above (or a mix of categories) should be sent to the Vice President for Academic Affairs/Dean of Faculty who will send them to the Instruction Committee for review and recommendation. Deadlines will be announced each year. Grant monies are for activities that take place no sooner than July 1 of the next budget year, and normally should be expended within the fiscal year.

The following steps, constituting a professional development planning process, must be taken in applying for, then carrying out, Faculty Professional Development Grants:

1. Write Profile and Develop a Specific Twelve-Month Plan

Write a professional development profile for the next two to three years. In a few paragraphs describe what you envision as the nature of your evolution as a professional during this time. As a scholar and educator, how do you see your development during this period?

Describe specific activities to be carried out during the grant period (normally no more than one year) for which you are applying for money. How do these activities fit into your professional development as described above.

2. Work With Advisory-Support Group

Select a minimum of three colleagues to function in advisory-support capacities by meeting with you as a group at least once. The purpose of the meeting would be to review your Profile and revise your Twelve-Month Plan. This interaction can be very useful in fine-tuning your plan and enlightening colleagues of your professional plans. These colleagues should sign the final version of the Twelve-Month Plan.

3. Apply for Funding

Send the completed Profile and Plan to the Vice President for Academic Affairs/Dean of Faculty by the appropriate deadline.

4. Carry Out the Planned Prospect

5. Have Final Meeting with Advisory-Support Group

You should meet with your advisory-support group when your project has been completed. The purpose of this meeting is to convey to colleagues new findings, perspectives, questions or directions, etc., which have emerged from implementing your Twelve-Month Plan.

6. Prepare Summary Report

You are responsible for compiling a brief summary of the actual activities you undertook and the benefits derived from these activities. Send this summary to the Dean and the Instruction Committee.

Travel to Professional Meetings

The College attempts to meet reasonable requests for professional travel. Attendance at professional meetings can enhance individual professional growth and contribute to the enhancement of the academic program of the College. Guidelines for College support of such travel are described below.

Policies Applicable to All Professional Travel -- Regardless of which travel program is involved (see below), expense reimbursement will be limited to transportation (commercial, or personal car at 20 cents per mile), registration fees, and a per diem of $60 per night away from the campus. Although figured on a per night basis, and thus fundamentally a reimbursement for the lodging that is required for travel, the per diem may be applied toward meal costs also.

Faculty members who wish to apply for travel funds should submit the travel request form, available in the Academic Affairs Office, appropriate to the travel program involved (see below). Approval of the request will enable the individual to make travel reservations and take other concrete steps in preparation for the travel. Airline tickets may be charged to a College credit card through the Academic Affairs Office, but where travel approval has been secured in advance, reimbursement to the individual after the travel is completed may be obtained. In any case, on return from the travel, an expense report form must be submitted for approval by the Dean. (A special form is required for the general program of professional travel; otherwise the standard College form is to be used.) Appropriate receipts must be presented. Cash advances may be requested from the accounting office. In making airline reservations, faculty are asked to divide their business among local travel agencies.

IV-4

Northrup Library
Linfield College
McMinnville, Oregon

Three Programs and Sources of Funds For Travel to Professional Meetings. – The following three programs are available to regular faculty in support by the College of travel to professional meetings:

Departmentally-Budgeted Funds for "Local" Travel

Funds are available in departmental budgets to assist with travel to meetings within the local area that normally do not require overnight stays. It is the responsibility of the department chairperson to see that expenditures do not exceed the amount budgeted. Although provided on a per-person basis, departments may decide to assign these monies by other means as they see fit.

Dean's Travel Fund for Presentations at Professional Meetings

Funds are available from the Academic Affairs Office to support travel to important national meetings for significant scholarly participation by faculty members. First priority is given to those who are traveling to deliver a substantive paper, especially when the paper is invited. Second priority is given to those who will chair a major panel or who must attend In the capacity of officer of the professional association. Third priority funding permitting) is given to those who will officially represent the College so as to benefit the institution in a concrete way. Since funds are limited, support will normally be limited to one meeting each year per faculty member. Requests for funds are made through department chairpersons in response to the Dean's call for such requests in the early part of the fall semester. There is no guarantee funds will remain for requests made later in the year.

Dean's Travel Fund for General Faculty Professional Travel ("$500 Fund")

Subject to availability of funding, subventions will be available from the Academic Affairs Office for simple attendance at national or regional scholarly or professional meetings or for other professional travel to further the capacities of the faculty member in teaching and related scholarship. The intent is to support such travel every second year per faculty member in an amount up to $500. The following procedures and guidelines apply in the two-year cycle, 1993-94 and 1994-95.

1. The purpose of the program is to enable a faculty participant to learn about or contribute to developments in his or her field(s), including curriculum and pedagogy as well as research, through professional travel, where such travel gives promise of enhancing the individual's professional contributions to the programs of the College in ways that cannot otherwise be accomplished. The individual will be responsible for using institutional funds in accord with this statement; prior approval of the purpose of trips will not be required.

2. Although individuals and departments may wish to coordinate travel plans under this program with travel under the above travel program which requires being on the program of a meeting, there is no general policy linkage between the programs. In other words, while everyone is encouraged to participate in the new program, the other program continues in force as an incentive to sharing one's work with external colleagues.

3. Funding is sufficient to provide a subvention of up to $500 every second year to each full-time faculty person who is on a renewable (non-temporary) contract. Non-adjunct employees whose contracts include a faculty portion of at least 0.50 FTE will be eligible on a prorata basis. Expenses for some people who are eligible in a given year may well come in at less than the maximum for which they are eligible; if so, the unused balances will be divided before the books close on that year among those who incurred eligible expenses exceeding $500 while traveling with subventions. However, since such additional reimbursement will depend on the experience of the particular year and thus is not guaranteed, the individual whose eligible expenses exceed $500 must be prepared to absorb this permanently in the event extra funds are not available. Because funds do not carry forward from one fiscal year to the next, travel under this program cannot be postponed into the next year.

4. Allowable expenses are coach air fare (with an expected attempt in each case to obtain "budget rates"), registration fees, ground transportation to and from airports, and a $60 per diem (based on number of lodging nights whether or not used for lodging).

5. The Dean of Faculty, working closely with department chairpersons, will set up the schedule of which faculty will be eligible in what years. At least for the first two-year cycle, deviations from this schedule will not be permitted.

6. A faculty member who is eligible to travel under this program in a given year will initiate the process of funding each trip by completing a special completed travel authorization form. If records show a balance in that year's allocation for that individual, permission will be granted to proceed with the travel, including booking airline reservations.

7. In addition to the final financial "settling up" that occurs upon return from a trip, the faculty member will provide a brief narrative report (generally no more than a page) identifying the nature of the trip and describing outcomes (ideas, insights, developments, contacts, etc.) that may contribute to the individual's work or the academic program at Linfield. This report will be sent to the department chairperson with a suggestion that it might be the subject of a departmental discussion, and will be placed also in the individual's evaluation file.

Manuscript Preparation

To stimulate publication and the presentation of scholarly papers at significant regional and national meetings, manuscript assistance will be available through the Office of the Vice President for Academic Affairs/Dean of Faculty.

When research is completed on a paper or monograph, application may be made to the Dean for funds to cover final typing and copying. It is assumed that all drafts and other preliminary work will be done by the faculty member at his or her own expense.

The work supported should be a contribution to the profession which reflects positively upon the College as well as the faculty member.

Once approval is secured, the faculty member should first try to engage the services of a typist already on the staff. Work would be done outside of normal working hours and compensated at $6.50 per hour. A fixed sum will be approved in advance, and a bill must be presented by the typist or copier. If no such persons are available, then non-Linfield persons may be engaged at the same rate.

Informal Sharing With Colleagues From Other Campuses

The College will assist an academic department in bringing colleagues in the same field at another college to Linfield for an afternoon or evening of informal sharing. This normally would involve a meal. Applications should be sent to the Vice President for Academic Affairs/Dean of Faculty.

Professional Development Workshops and Discussions

The College plans to continue offering significant workshops from time to time on major topics related to the work of significant members of the Linfield faculty. The same is true of discussions for smaller groups, less formal and more flexible than the larger workshops. Topics for either workshops or discussions should be submitted to the Dean or the Coordinator of Faculty Development.

Departmental Consultants

If departments wish to engage consultants to assist in curricular and special instructional development problems, they may apply to the Dean. The problem should be one which cannot adequately be dealt with by Linfield personnel, and should be consistent with curricular policy and of direct relevance to improving the quality of departmental offerings.

Changes in Professional Emphasis

A faculty member who wishes to consider a shift in his or her professional emphasis should discuss this with the department head and the Dean. If this is judged to be in the interest of the College, a program may be developed and funded, at least in part, by the College. For example, a faculty member might arrange a summer study program at the University of Oregon to provide a solid basis for teaching in a somewhat different area of the current discipline, or, in some cases in a different discipline. If the change in emphasis is approved, the study project would be pursued by application for a Faculty Professional Development Grant.

Faculty Exchange

In a time of decreased mobility of faculty, both the individual Linfield faculty member and the College may benefit from a faculty exchange in which the Linfield faculty member exchanges places with a faculty member from another institution for a semester or academic year. Proposals for such exchanges will be considered on a case by case basis, with due attention to the qualifications of the visiting faculty member and the impact of the exchange on the academic program.

For an approved exchange, each institution would continue to pay salary and benefits to its own faculty member while that person is teaching at the other institution. As funds permit, the College will provide a "dislocation allowance" to the Linfield faculty member in recognition of the costs incurred in relocating for a short period of time (housing, travel, etc.).

The College provides assistance in arranging exchanges through its membership in the Faculty Exchange Center located at Franklin and Marshall College. This membership permits Linfield faculty (and administrators) to list their availability for exchanges in a published national registry. This registry is also a source of information about faculty elsewhere who are seeking an exchange. Interested faculty should discuss the possibility with the Vice President for Academic Affairs/Dean of Faculty and with their department chairperson, and may wish to consult with the Coordinator of Faculty Development.

Sabbatical Leaves and Leaves Without Pay

Please see material on these programs in Chapter III.

the following year's appointment. If an offer of employment is made for the following year (for those faculty members who have not received tenure), this information as well as the salary terms for the next year are included. To accept, the faculty member signs and returns one copy to the Office of the Provost. This action constitutes a mutual agreement, binding upon both parties for the period involved.

The payroll is prepared by the Payroll Office and any questions of a specific nature should be referred to that source.

3.   Termination

When the appointment of a faculty member terminates, he/she will coordinate with the Business Office arrangements for his/her insurance and other benefits, and turn in all University property.

4.   Leave of Absence

When a faculty member will be on leave during any part of the following academic year, he/she should contact the Business Office to make arrangements for the continuation of some of his/her benefits and other related matters.

G.   Policy Statement on Appointment of Librarians[1]

Librarians make a significant contribution to the educational program and general academic life of a college. They have an important responsibility for developing library collections, for bibliographical control over these collections, for informing students about library resources and uses, and for advising faculty in the use of the collection. They answer questions, compile bibliographies, and strive to improve library processes and practices. Their work involves high-level skills of communication, analysis, organization, and follow-through, among others. It requires trained intelligence and graduate professional education.

Given the close involvement of librarians in support of the faculty's teaching and the student's learning, professional librarians at Ohio Wesleyan will be voting members of the Faculty and will be eligible for election to the committees of that body. Because the duties and responsibilities of librarians are significantly different in important respects from those of the classroom faculty, appointments of librarians will not necessarily be governed by the terms and conditions applicable to classroom faculty, but will, except as explicitly noted herein, be

---

[1] The policies described do not apply to librarians who have been appointed as faculty librarians before the 1982-83 academic year. The term 'librarian' in this policy statement refers to all other professional librarians—professional library staff with graduate library degrees.

governed by those of the non-faculty professional staff of the
University. In addition to membership in the faculty body as noted
above, the following special terms and conditions will be applicable to
librarians.

1. Performance appraisals of librarians, including the Director of
    Libraries, will make use of several sources of information
    including a self-report, evaluations from librarian-colleagues,
    and evaluation by library patrons. The Library Subcommittee of the
    Committee on Teaching and Learning will determine appropriate
    procedures for evaluation by patrons. Using the above information
    and consulting with the Director of Libraries except, of course,
    when his or her own case is involved, the Provost shall make final
    personnel recommendations to the President.

2. The normal highest degree for professional librarians is the
    master's degree in library science. Librarians entering employ-
    ment with this degree will be paid at the level of entering
    teaching faculty with comparable training and experience. They
    will also participate in salary increases on the same basis as
    faculty members and other professional staff.

3. Librarians will be eligible to apply for paid study leaves after
    six years since start of service or since the last leave. Such
    leaves will not be automatic, but must be approved by the Provost
    upon recommendation of the Director of Libraries in consultation
    with the Library Subcommittee of the Committee on Teaching and
    Learning for projects which promise to advance the contribution of
    the library to the academic life of the institution. They normally
    will be granted for an eight-week period in the summer, which
    period shall be in addition to the usual one-month annual vaca-
    tion.

4. A librarian may be the instructor of record for credit-bearing
    student work upon approval of the Provost who will make an
    appropriate appointment on the recommendation of the department or
    program which has responsibility for the course(s) involved. On
    the recommendation of the Faculty Personnel Committee, this
    appointment may be a continuing departmental "courtesy appoint-
    ment." In other cases it will be for the academic term of the
    course(s) involved.

5. A librarian may use the appropriate appeal process in the Faculty
    Handbook for a case he or she believes involves violation of his
    or her academic freedom.

promises to enhance the quality of the individual's teaching.

3. Special Released Time for Scholarly Production

    a. In preparation of the University budget certain monies shall
        be set aside in a special account for the express purpose of
        encouraging faculty members with recognized expertise to
        enter into grant-supported research or outstanding creative
        endeavors requiring rigorous commitments. These funds shall
        be adequate to replace one faculty member per year for one
        semester paid leave. The funds shall provide a replacement
        up to the average salary level of a full professor, should
        this be necessary;

    b. The total remuneration during any semester for which reduced
        load is granted, or during any semester for which special
        leave is granted, shall not exceed the regular salary of the
        grantee;

    c. Support under this program shall be reserved for major and
        unique projects and shall meet the following criteria;

        (1) normally, consideration will be given to those who
             have invested at least two years in their projects;

        (2) the project must hold promise for significant
             contribution to the University community;

        (3) the project must entail commitment to respon-
             sibilities, duties, time schedules or other obliga-
             tions which cannot be accommodated within the
             framework of our regular leave program.

    d. Application for support shall be made jointly by the faculty
        member and the department chairperson who will submit to the
        Provost a statement indicating the special nature of the
        proposed activity, the unique conditions requiring special
        leave, and a plan setting for the time span for which the
        request is made as well as a proposal for coverage of
        teaching and other responsibilities;

    e. This program shall be administered by the Provost in con-
        sultation with Faculty Personnel Committee. It shall be
        understood that applicants holding grants will not seek paid
        leave in violation of the conditions of their grants.

4. Retraining Leaves

    Upon application, full-time faculty members may be granted up to
    one year of paid leave to undergo professional retraining to equip
    them to take on new assignments which contribute to, or are the
    result of, reduction in faculty positions. The Provost, in

Franklin F. Moore Library
Rider College
Lawrenceville, New Jersey

Agreement 1991-1994 between Rider College and the Rider College Chapter of the American Associationof University Professors, Article XXV, "Workload," p. 95.

6. Professional Development Days

In addition to assignments within the Library, the responsibilities of professional librarians include professional development and scholarly activities. To support the professional development and scholarly activities of professional librarians, the College shall provide members of the faculty five (5) paid professional development days during the first and second years of this Agreement and an additional two (2) paid professional development days during the third year of this Agreement. Such professional days shall be scheduled during June, July, and August.

Agreement 1991-1994 between Rider College and the Rider College Chapter of the American Association of University Professors, Article XXVII, "Faculty Development," p. 101-103.

D.   Summer Fellowships

1. Eligibility

All full-time members of the bargaining unit shall be eligible to make application for summer fellowships, except that full-time bargaining unit members who are receiving a stipend from another source to cover living expenses during the summer months or who are engaged in teaching more than one (1) course during the summer (excluding the Minimester) shall not be eligible for summer fellowships. Full-time members of the faculty who do not receive summer fellowships shall have priority for the assignment of summer teaching. Members of the Faculty Research and Patent Committee shall not be eligible for summer fellowships during the term for which they were elected.

2. Number and Amount of Awards

During the first year of this Agreement, the College shall allot twenty-three (23) summer fellowships to full-time bargaining unit members, subject to the receipt of applications for such fellowships and subject to the evaluation and determination of merit for each such application by the Faculty Research and Patent Committee. The number of fellowships shall be increased to twenty-five (25) during the second year of this Agreement and twenty-six (26) during the third year of this Agreement. Such fellowships shall carry a stipend of $3,885 during the first year of this Agreement, $4,100 during the second year of this Agreement, and $4,345 during the third year of this Agreement. Such stipends shall be payable in equal installments in July and August.

If the reipient of a summer fellowship is a member of the library faculty, the recipient shall receive twenty (20) days compensatory time off. The recipient shall propose a schedule for such compensatory time. If the Director of Library Services disagrees with the schedule proposed by the recipient, he/she shall respond in writing with an alternative schedule. If the recipient and the Director of Library Services are unable to agree on a schedule, the matter shall be referred to the Provost for a determination.

3. Conditions

Summer fellowships may be awarded for scholarly study, research, and writing that will contribute to the professional development of full-time bargaining unit members and be of benefit to the College. Recipients shall be obligated to return to the College for at least one (1) full year of service after receiving the summer fellowship. Within ninety (90) days of the opening of the Fall semester following receipt of a summer fellowship, a recipient shall be required to submit to the President, with copies to the Provost, the faculty member's dean or supervisor, and his/her department or staff, a written report including a description of the initial proposal and a summary o the activities undertaken during the fellowship. The Provost will keep said reports on file and make them available to the Chairperson of the Faculty Research and Patent Committee upon request.

4. Procedures

Faculty Research and Patent Committee shall select from among the pool of applicants twenty-three (23) full-time bargaining unit faculty members during the first year of this Agreement, twenty-five (25) during the second year of this Agreement, and twenty-six (26) during the third year of this Agreement to recommend for summer fellowships. The Committee will also recommend three (3) alternates, who are full-time bargaining unit members, in ranked order, in case one (1) or more of the selected faculty members is unable to accept the fellowship. The Chairperson of the Committee shall forward a copy of the recommendations together with the relevant applications from the recommended bargaining unit members to the Provost prior to its final transmittal to the President.

5. Appeal

Bargaining unit members may appeal the failure of the Faculty Research and Patent Committee to follow the required procedure hereunder, but no appeal may be filed on the basis that the Faculty Research and Patent Committee has made an error in judging the merit of any proposal. The bargaining unit members of the College Academic Policy Committee shall hear all such procedural appeals and shall render a final decision. As to remedy, the bargaining unit members of the College Academic Policy Committee shall be limited to remanding the matter back to the Faculty Research and Patent Committee with specific procedural instructions. Except as set out hereafter, appeals regarding the actions of the President under this Article shall be limited to an alleged failure by the President to follow the required procedure and shall be processed under the grievance and arbitration provisions of this Agreement as to the basis for any such deviation from these recommendations.

6. Notification

The College shall notify recipients of summer fellowships by March 18 of the academic year preceding the summer for which the awards are applicable if the Provost has received the recommendations from the Faculty Research and Patent Committee, as aforesaid, by the preceding March 1.

West Liberty State College
STAFF DEVELOPMENT POLICIES

The Staff Development Commmittee supports the professional development of classified employees. The committee recognizes the need for staff to improve skills and to pursue further education or other activities to help them to upgrade their abilities for their positions.

Goals

The primary goal of the Staff Development Committee is to extend and enhance the abilities of the individual.

Staff Development encompasses a number of broad areas including but not limited to: career development, job-related skills, instructional development, and personal development. The Staff Development Committee will support a wide range of activities which promote improvement in these areas and which will contribute to the overall performance of classified employees.

The Staff Development Committee will seek and provide funding to eligible classified employees to use for such activities as: career development, job related skills, on-campus workshops, professional meetings, conferences, and seminars designed to upgrade skills and to acquire knowledge.

Policy Regarding Staff Development

.   Purposes of Staff Development

West Liberty State College Staff Development Committee recognized the need for members of the classified staff to improve their skills and pursue further education or any other activities that will keep them abreast of developments in their respective areas of responsibility. The Staff Development Committee will support the staff in pursuing ways to upgrade their skills. It will seek to administer all decisions regarding the distribution of funds fairly and equitably.

The Staff Development Committee recognizes the role classified staff play in the delivery of services at West Liberty State College. The Committee understands that the knowledge and skills of classified staff need to be developed, maintained, supported and renewed and will strive to accomplish these objectives.

I. Definition of Staff Development

Staff Development encompasses a number of broad areas, including but not limited to: career development, job related skills, instructional development, and personal development. The Committee will support those activities which promote improvement in these areas and which will contribute to the overall performance of the classfied staff.

II. Staff Eligibility and Participation

Eligibility - Any person who is a classified employee of West Liberty State College is eligible for staff development.

Participation - Staff members are responsible for improving their job effectiveness. The West Liberty State College Staff Development Committee is responsible for encouraging and motivating staff members to participate in staff development activities.

Orientation and Mentoring Programs

CARDINAL
STRITCH
COLLEGE

V A L U E S &
V I S I O N S
Faculty Mentoring

The mentoring of all new full- and part-time faculty has made a widespread and powerful impact at Cardinal Stritch College. It is an impact felt by new faculty, mentors, department chairpersons and, most definitely, students.

The mission of the college highlights the expectation for high-quality instruction. With "Teaching Excellence" as a goal, every attempt is made to provide new faculty with non-evaluative, immediate and on-going assistance.

Instructors new to the campus (mentees) are carefully paired for two semesters with experienced colleagues (mentors) who have earned reputations as effective teachers and communicators. The Mentoring Program is initiated with a thorough orientation to the campus and the college's mission programs and policies.

Orientation to all aspects of faculty life is the major goal for the first semester of mentoring; it is a rapport-building stage designed to support the mentees in becoming as comfortable as possible as soon as possible. It is felt that once the routine, mechanical concerns are alleviated and the myriad of questions are answered, the mentees can concentrate on their major responsibility – quality instruction. Frequent informal meetings, usually over lunch, set the stage for subsequent classroom observations. The mentor's teaching serves as a role model for the mentee and, in return, the mentee can gain valuable feedback and suggestions following an observation by the mentor.

Coaching the mentee to higher levels of teaching effectiveness is the major focus for the second semester. It affords the mentee the support and resources necessary to refine and improve instruction. Two or more observations of the mentee are scheduled and followed with conferences. The Mentoring Program's greatest contribution is that it has faculty talking about and striving for effective teaching practices.

6801 NORTH YATES ROAD
MILWAUKEE, WISCONSIN 53217-3985
414-352-5400 FAX 414-351-7516

Faculty Mentoring Program - 89

The two semesters of mentoring are followed by Peer Coaching, a perpetual continuation of teachers coaching teachers. It gives colleagues the opportunity for ongoing support and feedback that is critical for continued growth. Colleagues choose partners to work with over an unspecified period of time. New partnerships are forged when faculty form new personal goals for instruction.

Additional Significant Aspects for the Mentoring Program

* Mentors and mentees are most frequently matched across departmental boundaries which is considered a positive in developing collegiality across campus.

* A confidentiality policy protects the mentor-mentee relationship. Principle evaluators, the Department Chairpersons, are not privy to the mentors' information regarding new faculty.

* The college provides .25 FTE released time for a faculty member to coordinate all aspects of the Mentoring Program and serve as a troubleshooter and liaison between the various parties. All mentors are paid a stipend.

Evaluation responses praise the Mentoring Program as an overwhelming success. Students are the main benefactors. Student achievement is the primary reason for the emphasis on quality instruction. Has mentoring made a difference? One would certainly receive an enthusiastic, affirmative answer at Cardinal Stritch College.

Judith DuMez
Judith DuMez, Assistant Professor
Director, Mentoring Program

SUBJECT: Employee Orientation

PURPOSE: To orient newly hired employees to co-workers, programs, and policies
of the college.

POLICY: The college shall consistently provide orientation for all new
employees to help them identify with the mission of the college and
become positively incorporated into the college community.

PRACTICES &
PROCEDURES:

I. Director of Personnel's Responsibility

A. The Director of Personnel shall complete the New Employee
Information Form and give it to the employee as well as
placing a copy in her/his personnel file.

B. The Director of Personnel shall give an Employee
Handbook to each new employee.

C. The Director of Personnel shall notify (with the
New Personnel Release Form) the Director
of Public Relations that a new employee has been
hired. Public Relations shall obtain appropriate
biographical information for a news release.

II. Immediate Supervisor's Responsibility

A. The supervisor shall introduce the employee to all
the other departmental co-workers as well as other
employees with whom the person shall be working.

B. The supervisor shall give the employee a current
job description outlining the duties and responsibilities of the position.

C. The supervisor shall apprise the employee of her/his
relationship to the department's function, goals,
and practices as they relate to the mission of the
college.

III. The P.E.O.P.L.E. Responsibility

A. P.E.O.P.L.E. staff shall conduct a campus tour to
explain briefly the various office's functions and to
provide a general introduction for each new employee.

B. P.E.O.P.L.E. shall offer a new employee orientation
seminar periodically. The orientation shall include
but is not limited to the following:

1. greetings and general remarks by the President
outlining the college's philosophy and mission;

2. a description of the college by the staff of
admissions, academic affairs, business affairs,
and student affairs;

3. orientation to employee programs offered by
P.E.O.P.L.E.;

4. question and answer session about new employees'
concerns.

MENTORING

The mentor's duties during the first three days of orientation are noted in the checklist; however, after this time, there are no set rules to follow. It is most likely that the mentor, unlike the supervisor, will serve as the _informal_ resource person for the new employee, helping that person to "learn the ropes." The mentor should try to have daily, if not more frequent, contact with the new employee and should be an integral part of the training program.

In addition, the mentor should act as a social bridge for the new employee by inviting him/her to activities with or without staff outside of work, or by encouraging other staff to involve the new person in social activities. The mentor could also serve as a community resource person by informing the new employee of local events, festivals, etc. and by answering questions about the community.

It is possible that, for any number of reasons, the new employee and the mentor will not establish a close rapport. If this seems to be the case, the mentor should be forthright in acknowledging the situation and should take the initiative in finding another staff member as a replacement.

It is readily apparent that the mentor plays an important part in orienting the new staff member. The supervisor should, therefore, be very careful in selecting the right person for the role. The following is a list of qualities to consider in choosing a good mentor:

- patience

- good communicator

- good "people" skills

- positive attitude

- superior performer

- good delegator

- sense of humor

- able to explain concepts in different ways

CSB/SJU JOINT LIBRARY

ORIENTATION PROGRAM FOR NEW LIBRARY STAFF

New employees often enter a job with an inadequate introduction to their working environment. They may be trained in the specific functions covered by the job description; however, they may not have the opportunity to discover how they and their job fit into the larger organizational picture. This lack of context can lead to decreased job performance, stress, low morale, dissatisfaction with the job and the organization, and eventually, departure from the organization.

The purpose of the orientation program is to help new library employees avoid these pitfalls and thrive in their jobs. By the end of the program, employees should have a sense of accomplishment in several areas: they should be acquainted with the mission and goals of the libraries; they should be aware of the many resources and services which the libraries have to offer; they should have a strong sense of the spiritual, educational, and historical context in which they are working; and finally, they should feel at ease and an integral part of the library staff and academic community.

The orientation program is meant to supplement the orientation to institutional policies and employee benefits provided by the personnel office. It should also be implemented along with a training program for the specific job being filled.

To set the program in motion, the associate director for the area concerned, the employee's immediate supervisor (if different from the associate director) and the mentor will meet a week or two before the employee arrives. Using the checklist provided, they will develop an individualized orientation program. This group will also develop the training program. All members of the group should retain copies of the programs, and the supervisor should also send copies to the employee before arrival.

During the orientation process, the group should get together for a mid-way assessment of the program. After six months, as noted in the checklist, the supervisor will interview the new employee about the orientation program. The group should convene after this session for a final assessment.

Alcuin Library
Saint John's University/College of Saint Benedict
Collegeville, Minnesota

ORIENTATION CHECKLIST

parations by supervisor

_ Select a staff mentor

_ Make sure that desk is stocked with necessary supplies (including a loaf of
Johnnie or Bennie bread, complimentary copy of the Rule, course catalog, and J-
Book or EveryWoman's Guide)

_ Set up VAX account (including a "welcome" mail message) and arrange VAX
workshop with Microcomputing, occurring on: _____(date) at _____(time)

_ Add new staff member to phone list and distribute

_ Order name tag and/or nameplate

_ Arrange for introduction by Director or Associate Director at next staff
assembly meeting, occurring on _____(date) at _____(time)

first three days

e: S = Supervisor's responsibility to carry out or arrange
M = Mentor's responsibility to carry out or arrange

1

_ Visit personnel office **S**

_ Introduction to co-workers and mentor **S**

_ In-depth tour of "home" library **M**

_ Meet with associate director for discussion of department function and
organization. Receive copy of annual report **S**

_ Lunch at CSB Cafeteria or SJU Refectory (paid) **M**

_ Review job description and go over responsibilities and expectations **S**

_ Go over job-related departmental procedures (e.g., pay, holidays, breaks, hours,
timecards, overtime) **S**

_ Meet with mentor to discuss other problems (e.g., keys, doors, supplies, schedule
forms, copiers) and questions which have arisen during the day **M**

Alcuin Library
Saint John's University/College of Saint Benedict
Collegeville, Minnesota

Day 2

_____ In-depth tour of "home" campus **M**
_____ Review library policies **S**
_____ Review performance appraisal process **S**
_____ Meet with director for discussion of libraries' role in the
        institutions and employee's role in the libraries **S**
_____ Start job training **S**

Day 3

_____ Tour other library and campus **M**
_____ Get-acquainted meeting with staff at other library **M**
_____ Tour of HMML **M**
_____ Receive copy of <u>Library Basics</u> workbook **S**
_____ Receive bibliography of books about CSB/SJU **S**
_____ Watch videos on CSB and SJU **S**

<u>Later meetings with supervisor</u>

After 2 weeks (Date:)
_____ Meet with new employee and -

   - check understanding of responsibilities and procedures
   - check comfort level and give opportunity to ask questions

After 4 weeks (Date:)
_____ Meet to discuss progress and answer questions

After 8 weeks (Date:)
_____ Evaluate progress, set objectives for improvement, and answer questions

After 6 months (Date:)
_____ Evaluate employee performance
_____ Set performance goals
_____ Discuss areas of needed growth
_____ Interview employee about orientation program (Give copy of evaluation form
        before meeting)

Alcuin Library
Saint John's University/College of Saint Benedict
Collegeville, Minnesota

ORIENTATION EVALUATION

order to assist us in making the orientation process as helpful and pleasant as possible, this
aluation form. Your supervisor will schedule a time with you to discuss your experience of
e orientation process.

In what ways was the orientation process helpful to you?

Please rate the following aspects of the process:

	Very Helpful	Somewhat Helpful	Not Helpful
Staff "mentor"	_____	_____	_____
Tours of the libraries	_____	_____	_____
Tours of the institutions	_____	_____	_____
Library skills workbook	_____	_____	_____
Readings	_____	_____	_____
Videos	_____	_____	_____
Committee assignment	_____	_____	_____

omments:

In what ways could the orientation process be improved?

Needs/Interest Surveys, Programming, and Program Evaluation Forms

Training and Development Committees are planning a series of Spring seminars. What we would like now, is which of these seminars would you be interested in attending, provided money and instructors available. Please rate your top five from the list below, with one (1) being the most important to you. may also write in other choices!

Budget Preparation/Implementation
Care Planning/Dressing for success
Conflict Resolution
Creativity/Motivation
Decisions Making and Problem Solving
Developing Employee Participation
EEO/AA Issues
Effective Communication Skills
Effective Parenting
Handling Difficult People
Interpreting Financial Printouts & Reports
Job Expectations - Money is not the only reward
Leadership Skills
Managing Family & Work Conflicts
Participative Management Skills
Personal Financial Planning
Public Contact
Safety Programs
Sexual Harassment
Supervisory Skills
Teambuilding
Telephone Techniques
Time Management
Trust Building
Women in Management

Please check all training you would be interested in.

Computer Training

Lotus, 1,2,3	___ Beginner	___ Intermediate	___ Advanced
Word Perfect	___ Beginner	___ Intermediate	___ Advanced
PC SAS	___ Beginner	___ Intermediate	___ Advanced

Microsoft Works
Symphony
Pagemaker
MS/DOS
D/Base
Other (Please specify _____)

Captain John Smith Library
Christopher Newport University
Newport News, Virginia

Personnel Policy

____ Classification
____ Employee Counseling
____ Employee Relations
____ Departmental Orientation (after New Employee Orientation, where to go for travel questions,   purchasing, etc.)
____ Fair Labor Standards Act
____ Leave Policy
____ Performance Evaluation
____ Personnel Programs Offered by the State
____ Personnel Selection
____ Standards of conduct

Departmental Training

____ Budget
____ Purchasing
____ Travel
____ Other

How many training programs have you attended, since your employment with this College?
____

How many classes have you completed under the tuition waiver program? ____

Have you ever been denied a training request? yes or no

What reason was given for your denial?

Would you be willing to serve on a committee that plans social activities?
If so, please contact the personnel office.

Comments concerning Training and Development

Please return this form in the enclosed self-addressed envelope no later than
Thank you for completing this survey!

STAFF DEVELOPMENT QUESTIONNAIRE FOR
LIBRARY FACULTY

The purpose of this questionnaire is to gain information on the staff development
concerns and needs of the library faculty.

Please answer the following questions:

1.   Please rank the following individually as to which library faculty staff
     development activities the College should support in terms of paid release
     time and funding:

     (KEY: 1=essential to offer full support; 2=should offer at least partial support;
     3=would be nice, but not essential; 4=should not support)

_____   library-related workshops within driving distance
_____   library-related workshops that require air travel
_____   consortium activities within driving distance
_____   consortium activities that require air travel
_____   library-related conferences outside of our 1 faculty benefit conference
          per year
_____   conference fees for the 1 faculty benefit conference per year
_____   tuition for additional library school classes taken
_____   paid release time for additional library school classes taken
_____   tuition for additional non-library school courses taken when course(s)
          are demonstrated to be helpful for job-related tasks
_____   paid release time for additional non-library school courses taken when
          course(s) are demonstrated to be helpful for job-related tasks
_____   tuition for courses taken toward a college degree other than library or
          information science
_____   paid release time for courses taken toward a college degree other than
          library or information science
_____   library-related research/publication activities
_____   research/publication activities in disciplines other than library or
          information science
_____   support for research expenses during leave of absence
_____   support for library conferences during leave of absence
_____   support for travel expenses related to library work when on leave of
          absence
_____   paid leave or paid release time for work on dissertation
_____   paid release time while studying for comprehensive exams for
          advanced degree
_____   expenses for visits to other libraries to see how things are done
_____   OTHER: _____
_____   OTHER: _____

COMMENTS:

2. What are your concerns related to the present leave program available to library faculty?

3. What have you used as sources of funding for staff development activities in the past? Check off all that apply.

_____ The Vice President for Academic Affairs office for annual conference benefit
_____ The Dean of Faculty's office for research-related projects
_____ The Dean of Faculty's office for library-related workshops, etc.
_____ The library's travel fund
_____ OTHER: _____
_____ OTHER: _____
_____ OTHER: _____
_____ OTHER: _____
_____ OTHER: _____
_____ OTHER: _____

COMMENTS:

4. Please list in-house staff development workshops (topics) that you would like to see presented at the library.

5. Other staff development concerns:

STAFF DEVELOPMENT PROGRAM SURVEY

Please take some time and thought to advise us about your suggestions concerning staff development activities for the 1992/1993 academic year. Before you decide, you may wish to consider what we have done in the past and some suggestions that have been made for future programs.

Some Past Activities:
       Reports on A.L.A. meetings and programs
       Dr. Janice Fennell - Report on preservation/conservation of the Flannery O'Connor Manuscripts
       Dr. Frank Lowney - GC EduNet
       Dr. William I. Hair - discussion of his research/publication of The Kingfish and His Realm.   (Huey P. Long)
       Soviet Union and comparison of college life in the U.S. and the Soviet Union
       Dr. Helen Hill - GC services provided to handicapped students
       Dr. Yasys Tsiovkh - schools and family life in the Ukraine
       Dr. Zi Pei - Chinese history and stress relieving techniques
       Dr. Jim Newberry and Dr. Barbara Funke - Wellness Workshop

Some Suggestions for Future Programs:
       MS-Dos Workshops
       PeachNet Workshop
       Introduction to Law Reference
       Ergonomics and Computers in the Workplace
       Tour of GCTV and the renovated Media Services area
       DeskTop publishing tips
       Julia Flisch update - Robin Harris
       Planning for the library addition (this activity is planned for Spring break)

Your Suggestions:

Iowa Library Association/A.C.R.L. Staff Development Committee

STAFF DEVELOPMENT

Criteria for Success:

- Opportunities for continuing education across size & type of library
  - professional staff
  - nonprofessional staff
- Widespread participation
- Quality presenters
- Accessible and affordable programs
- Coordinating group for total program

Standards & Goals:

- Develop coordinating group
- Programs make "on the job" differences
- Funding available locally or through grants
- Provide programs of immediate interest
- Provide opportunities for exchanges, etc.
- Specified number of contact hours available to every staff member each year
- Use of appropriate technology for programs

Data Required:

- Number of contact hours/variety of programs available
- Percentage of staff participating
- Amount of funding available
- Evaluation of each program by participants for evaluation of total program
- Periodic survey of staff for program ideas

Alternative Methods:

- Work through library school as coordinating group (or committee of ILA/ACRL or coordinate with Regional System)
- encourage participation of non-professionals in a section of ILA/ACRL
- Variety of programs: visits; exchanges; video with facilitator; downlinking; workshops hands-on
- Use of mini-surveys on specific topics via fax (binding of periodicals, jobbers, etc.)
- Central files for library manuals, handbooks, procedures and exchange of such in house publications
- Central information source for money; establish statewide standard for requisit amount per person; develop scholarship fund; stress importance of tapping loca sources
- Availability of current staff programs: local, State Library catalog, ALA, othe associations
- Developing programs:
  - Share expertise with other states
  - Get training for local experts "train the trainers" (presentation style, speakin styles, teaching tips)

Iowa Library Association/A.C.R.L. Staff Development Committee
ILA/ACRL Staff Development Working Group Needs Survey

fter consulting with librarians and staff in your library, please indicate the interest in aving a staff development program in the areas listed below according to the following cale: **High importance - 1, Medium importance - 2, Some importance - 3, No mportance - 4.**

Job Skills
> Searching national databases _____

> Microcomputer training _____

> Word processing _____

> Spreadsheet _____

> Database management systems _____

> Online searching _____

> Using CD-ROMs _____

> Teaching skills _____

Management Skills
> Supervision
>> -Students _____

>> -Staff _____

>> -Librarians _____

> Time Management _____

> Financial resource management _____

> Team building _____

> Self Management (Team workgroups) _____

Awareness Programs
> Harassment _____

> Racial awareness _____

> Serving international students _____

> Serving students with disabilities _____

Iowa Library Association/A.C.R.L. Staff Development Committee

Communication Skills
    Professional image _____

    Telephone etiquette _____

    Conducting a meeting _____

    Giving a presentation _____

    Written communication _____

    Developing in-house publications _____

    Dealing with patrons _____

    Writing for public relations _____

    Grant proposal writing _____

Health Issues
    Wellness
        -Nutrition _____

        -Stress reduction _____

        -Exercise _____

    CPR _____

    First aid _____

Please indicate other interests. Also indicate ongoing programs at your library that you would consider sharing on a statewide basis. Use additional sheets if necessary.

List below your name, institution and address:

Please return this form by September 14, 1990 to : William K. Black, Assistant Director for Administrative Services and Personnel, 302 Parks Library, Iowa State University, Ames, IA 50011-2140.

****
LIBRAS CONTINUING EDUCATION PROGRAM
****

GUIDELINES

1.   **STATEMENT OF PURPOSE.** This program provides financial support in order to further the professional development of LIBRAS professional staff members so that benefits will accrue to LIBRAS in addition to the individual and her/his library.

2.   **TYPES OF ACTIVITIES COVERED.** This program covers the following activities but is not necessarily limited to them alone: attendance at conferences, meetings, workshops, and seminars: visits to individuals or institutions; and visits by individuals to LIBRAS libraries or staff.

3.   **ELIGIBILITY.** All LIBRAS staff members are eligible to apply. The applicant must have direct job responsibility for the subject area covered by the activity. Priority will be given to individuals who have not yet received LIBRAS funding. Ordinarily for a given conference, only one person per library will be funded.

4.   **ACCOUNTABILITY.** The applicant must consult with the Continuing Education Coordinator to determine the appropriate method of reporting to the membership on the results of the activity. If the awardee does not attend, for whatever reason, any advanced funding must be returned to LIBRAS. Anyone receiving continuing education assistance is required to write a report on the content of their continuing education experience and outline ways that they will share that experience with other LIBRAS members. These reports will be filed with the original application as an official LIBRAS document.

5.   **LOCATION.** If a particular activity is scheduled for several locations, the nearest location must be chosen.

PROCEDURES

1.   **APPLYING.** Submit a completed application, approved by the applicant's Director, together with a brochure or description of the activity, to the Continuing Education Coordinator.

2.   **DECISION-MAKING.** The Executive Committee via telefax will approve or reject the request and determine the amount of LIBRAS funding. The Executive Committee will determine what constitutes a "reasonable amount" for each request.

3.   **NOTIFICATION.** The Continuing Education Coordinator will notify the applicant of the Executive Committee's decision.

B.9

LIBRAS, INC.
North Central College
Naperville, Illinois

4. **PAYMENT.** Receipts and other documentation of covered expenditures after the activity has ended should be forwarded to the Continuing Education Coordinator. The Treasurer will forward payment to the applicant. In the event that a funded activity is canceled, the awardee is expected to return the funds immediately to LIBRAS, or inform LIBRAS of a definite date for the rescheduling of the event.

LIBRAS, a consortium of eighteen private academic libraries in the metro-Chicago area, was founded in 1965 to further interlibrary cooperation. To this end, LIBRAS has always promoted continuing education and the sharing of knowledge among staff of member libraries.

10/92rev.   B.10

110 - Continuing Education Program

Mercer/Monmouth/Ocean County
Academic Librarians Professional Development Meeting

SHOW AND TELL?
Presentation Skills for the Academic Librarian

Rider College Library, Lawrenceville, NJ

TUESDAY, MAY 19, 1992
9 AM-1 PM

Co-sponsored by
Rider College and Trenton State College Libraries

Contact: TSC: Pat Butcher   (609) 771-2433
           Rider: Lynn Livingston (609) 895-5637

30-9:00	Registration, Coffee and Donuts Room 338, Rider College Library
00	Welcome
10-10:20	*Active Learning in a Brief Encounter* **Dr. Myrna Smith,** New Jersey Institute for Collegiate Teaching and Learning, Seton Hall University
:20-10:30	Break
:30-11:40	*Librarians and Words: Public Speaking Skills and Library Instruction* **Dr.Frederick Turner,** Communication Department, Rider College
:40-11:50	Stretch Break
:50-12:50	*More than Words Can Say! Non-Verbal Communication and the College Librarian* **Dr. Myra Gutin,** Communications Department, Rider College
00	Dutch treat Luncheon (optional)

Mercer/Monmouth/Ocean County
Academic Librarians Professional Development Meeting

Mercer/Monmouth County
Academic Librarians
Professional Development Meeting

==

Please rate statements according to the following scale:

5 ="Excel.   4 ="V.Good   3 = Satisfactory   2 = Poor   1 = very poor

==

Overall usefulness of the seminar was...   5 4 3 2 1

Facilities & equipments used were.......   5 4 3 2 1

Applications to my own skills will be...   5 4 3 2 1

	SPEAKER 1	SPEAK 2	SPEAK 3
Contents of the speeches were.......	5 4 3 21	5 4 3 21	5 4 3 21
Style/Delivery of the speakers were..	5 4 3 21	5 4 3 21	5 4 3 21
Organization of material is..........	5 4 3 21	5 4 3 21	5 4 3 21
Opportunity for discuss./questions...	5 4 3 21	5 4 3 21	5 4 3 21

_____...   5 4 3 2 1

Should we form a consortium to meet on an semi and/or annual
        basis for programs like this? YES _____   NO_____
Would you be willing to host? YES_____

COMMENTS/SUGGESTIONS:

WHAT   TOPICS   WOULD   YOU   LIKE   TO   DISCUSS   IN   FUTURE

PROGRAMS?_____

_____

_____

_____

! ! ! THANK YOU ! ! !

112 - Evaluation

Murray Learning Resources Center
Messiah College
Grantham, Pennsylvania

Meeting Faculty at a New Place

An On-Campus Colleagues Conference

&

Soo K. Lee and Beth Mark • Messiah College • Grantham, Pennsylvania
(717) 766-2511 • Fax (717) 691-6042

Murray Learning Resources Center
Messiah College
Grantham, Pennsylvania

H elping teaching faculty keep current with new library technologies and services is a challenge both for the librarians and the faculty.

Librarians have found their participation in a campus-wide Colleagues Conference to be one solution to this problem. During this day-long conference, workshops are offered by campus faculty/staff on a wide variety of topics: ethnic cooking, computer searching, auto mechanics, tax preparation, etc. Faculty, staff, and administrators take a break from their normal routine to attend these workshops which foster the sharing of interests, skills, and scholarship among college personnel. Librarians have utilized this opportunity to offer workshops on CD-ROM products, the online catalog, FirstSearch Catalog, the Internet, and use of video equipment.

Librarians also have collaborated with teaching faculty and/or administrators in presenting workshops on such topics as critical thinking, alternatives to term papers, pathways through the scholarly publishing maze, and book reviews. Response to these workshops has been positive.

This session will provide a brief introduction to the Colleagues Conference. It will illustrate how the workshops help teaching faculty keep current with library technology, while enhancing librarians' interaction and collaboration with faculty members.

Planning a Colleagues Conference

Goals

Build community
Emphasize that learning is what we are all about
Give every member of the community an opportunity to teach
Affirm skills of administrators, faculty, and staff

Planning Group

Faculty Retreat Committee
Faculty Growth and Development Team
Associate Dean for Faculty Development
Personnel Director
Two or three staff members
Food Services representative
Conference Services Director

Planning Tips

· Obtain administrative support
· Choose a coordinator who is committed to the project and who cares about people – it requires
  a lot of time and organization
· Send call for proposals out early
· Tap on known resources if necessary
· Make it possible for all college employees to attend – time off from their regular work, free box
  lunch, etc.
· Be flexible – purposes may change over time
· Build in evaluation feedback for future planning

Selected Workshop Topics

FirstSearch via the Internet
Critical and Creative Thinking
Older Students – A Hidden Minority?
Korean Cooking
Finding and Using E-Mail Lists
Using the Online Catalog
Maintaining Lifelong Reading Habits
Pathways through the Publishing Maze
Improvisational Acting
Tired of Term Papers?
Bread Making
Educating the Exceptional Student
Time Management
Where There Is a Will There are Relatives
Geography Fun and Games
Competition vs Cooperation
Desktop Design
Computer Art

Window into Russia
Basic Athletic Prevention and Care
Confederate Soldiers in the Harrisburg Area
Federal, State, and Local Income Tax
Home Electrical Safety and Repairs
Rx for Healthy Plants
Music and Midi
Taking the Sting Out of Stress
Buying a Personal Computer
Death of Leisure
ProQuest – Elvis Cited on Database!
Why Students Act Like Students
Effective Communication
Getting Good Things Out of Bad Workers
Funeral Shopping
Weight Training for Beginners
Japanese Culture and Crafts

MESSIAH COLLEGE

memorandum

To: Messiah College Employees   *Subject:* *Colleagues Conference*

From: Dick Morrison, *Chair*, Faculty Affairs Committee
Paul Morgan, *Chair*, The Administrator & Staff Committee

The President's Cabinet has set January 8, 1993 as the date for Messiah College's Colleagues Conference. A part of the preparation for most conferences is a "call for papers," and that is indeed what this is.

As a member of the Messiah College community, you are invited to suggest a topic for a session that you would be willing to offer. We are looking for topics in all categories: professional, informational, inspirational, personal, and avocational. This is a prime opportunity for you to share with your colleagues here.

This paper is meant to solicit proposals for a session that you would be willing to offer. Our hope is to have those proposals collected no later than the middle of October. A committee will then compile the list and develop the conference program.

Topic:

Type of session:

Brief description:

Comments:

Your name: _____

116 - On-Campus Colleagues Conference

RICHMOND ACADEMIC LIBRARY COOPERATIVE
STAFF DEVELOPMENT NEEDS ASSESSMENT SURVEY QUESTIONNAIRE

The Richmond Academic Library Cooperative, which consist of libraries at Randolph-Macon College, Union Theological Seminary, University of Richmond, Virginia Commonwealth University, Virginia State University, and Virginia Union University is seeking information from RALC library staff members to assist in planning cooperative staff development activities. Your input will be valuable in assessing the topics you want and need to improve your performance. Please complete and return this questionnaire by October 1, 1987 to _____ _____.
Thank you.

This questionnaire is based on the following definition of Staff Development, to include:

1. Opportunities to expand library skills and knowledge in order to improve work performance and to increase understanding of library functions.

2. Opportunities that enable staff to improve skills not necessarily related to their present positions.

3. Programs presented in a variety of formats including series of courses, lectures, seminars, tours or other group activities, films, etc.   .

4. Programs to be attended by staff at their request and the discretion of the department head, assuming that commitments of the department are met.

5. Programs to be attended by student employees on their own time if their attendance does not displace a regular staff member.

Do you concur with this definition?   Yes_____   No_____   No Opinion_____.

Comments:

I.   Please check all that apply to your position:

   A. Length of employment in present position:

        Less than 1 year   _____
        1-3 years   _____
        4-5 years   _____
        6-10 years   _____ _____ _ _
        More than 10 years   _____

- 1 -

B. Administration _____
    Technical Services _____
    Public Services _____
    Other _____

C. Librarian _____
    Support Staff _____

D. Unit head (head of
    main department or
    branch) _____
    Supervisory _____
    Nonsupervisory _____

E. Full-time _____
    Part-time _____

1. Would you like staff development activities:
    _____a. to aid you in present position
    _____b. to aid in meeting requirements for other
           positions.
    _____c. other (specify)_____

2. Could your initial on-the-job training have been
    improved? (on the job training includes your
    orientation to the library and your department,
    initial job training by your supervisor or co-
    workers.)
            _____Yes   _____No

    How could this training have been improved?

3. Do you think the continous on-the-job training is
    adequate?

    Comments:

- 2 -

II.   Listed below are a number of possible staff development
ics which may be of interest. RALC wants to know the level of interes
have in these topics. This list is by no means exhaustive, we welcom
ments and suggestions for other programs.

Please circle your interest level or check the No interest
column for each topic.

Examples: No Interest   Medium   High
A.   Information on Optical Discs   0   1   2
B.   Training in Online Searching   0   1   2

                                        No Interest   Medium   High

1.   Library tours
     a. Branches of your library _____
     b. Other RALC Libraries_____

2.   Workshops, seminars, training
     presented by RALC staff or
     outside speaker._____
     a.   use of basic reference tools__
     b.   government documents_____
     c.   acquisitions_____
     d.   OCLC training_____
     e.   basics of automation_____
     f.   reference interview_____
     g.   preservation & conservation__
     h.   copyright laws_____
     i.   indexing_____
     j.   microcomputers for home
          and library use_____
     k.   library finance_____
     l.   personnel policies_____
     m.   student personnel policies___
     n.   interviewing and
          selecting employees____
     o.   EEO and Affirmative Action___
     p.   orienting new employees_____
     q.   training employees_____
     r.   motivation_____
     s.   conducting performance
          evaluations_____
     t.   personnel management_____
     u.   management by
          objectives_____
     v.   communication skills_____
     w.   time management_____
     x.   public relations_____
     y.   assertiveness training_____
     z.   resume writing_____

(list continued on the next page)

Needs Assessment Survey - 119

Richmond Academic Library Consortium
Richmond, Virginia

		No Interest	Medium	High
aa.	being evaluated			
bb.	being interviewed			
cc.	Writing for professional journals			
d.	safety & security programs			
e.	marketing			
ff.	planning(long range)			
gg.	planning (short range)			
hh.	planning (stategic)			
ii	future studies:			

(e.g. impact of changing
society on libraries,
future trends in library
services, etc.)

Other topics you are interested in :

_____
_____
_____

What are your top 3 choices from the above list:
1. _____
2. _____
3. _____

III. Please answer all questions.
    1.   Are you interested in attending staff development activities?
        Yes_____   No_____

    2.   Are you willing to spend your own time on staff development?
        Yes_____   No_____
        Your own money?_____ Please specify maximum amount: _____per session; _____per year.

    3.   Does your workload allow you to pursue a staff development program?   Yes_____   No_____

    4.   What kind of training would you like to see for your supervisor?
        (This is not limited to management training).

        Comments:

    5.   What kind of training would you like to see for your employees?

        Comments:

SUMMER STAFF DEVELOPMENT SURVEY

TO: Library Faculty and Staff

FROM: Continuing Education Committee
            Lucretia McCulley
            Dywana Saunders
            Marcia Whitehead
            Jane Young

SUBJECT: Summer Staff Development Programs

Summer will be here soon and the Continuing Education Committee is soliciting ideas for our summer staff development program. Please take a few minutes to complete our survey. Return to Lucretia McCulley's box by Friday, April 16. Thanks for your assistance.

TOPICS WHICH INTEREST YOU

___	Health & Nutrition	___	Music	___	Library Issues
___	Equipment Instruction	___	Literature	___	Other (list below)
___	Art & Architecture	___	Film		
___	Personal Development	___	Science		

LIST POSSIBLE FILM TITLES FOR LUNCH TIME VIEWING

_____

_____

LIST POSSIBLE LIBRARY TRIP DESTINATIONS

_____

_____

WHICH TIMES ARE MOST CONVENIENT FOR YOU?

_____

Boatwright Memorial Library
University of Richmond
Richmond, Virginia

WHICH DAYS ARE BEST FOR YOU TO ATTEND?

_____

HOW MANY SUMMER STAFF DEVELOPMENT SESSIONS DID YOU ATTEND LAST YEAR?

0   1-3   3-5   more than 5

LIST YOUR FAVORITE EVENT FROM THE PAST

_____

LIST YOUR LEAST FAVORITE EVENT

_____

OTHER IDEAS/SUGGESTIONS:

**Virginia Library Association. Continuing Education Committee
and the Virginia State Library and Archives**

Virginia Library Association
Continuing Education Committee
and the
Virginia State Library and Archives

CONTINUING EDUCATION & NEEDS ASSESSMENT

purpose of this survey is to help the CE Committee advise the Council of the
inia Library Association on providing quality continuing education programs
ed by its multi-type library audience. Your input will help us to determine the real
s of staff development. Continuing education programs should be designed to foster
development at all levels of staffing in all types of libraries.

ease check or complete as applicable all that apply to your position:

Type of library
Academic: Special: _____   Public _____   _____ School   Other
_2 year   _____ Corporate
_4 year   _____ Law
_4+ years   _____ Medical
              _____ Other (Please specify)

_ Other (Specify):

Type of position
_Administration   _____ Technical Services   _____ Public Services
_Other (Specify):

Category of paid personnel
Librarian: _____ Library Assistant   _____ Clerical   _____ Student
___ MLS
___ Certificate   _____ Other (Specify):

Level of supervision
_____ Library Director   _____ Unit Head   _____ Supervisory   _____ Other (Specify):

Hours of work
_____ Full time (over 37 hours/week)   _____ Part time   _____ Volunteer

vel of personal commitment

Would you like staff development activities -
___ To learn new skills   _____ For promotion   _____ To enhance career options
___ Other (Please Specify):

    B. Are you interested in --
        ____workshops   ___conferences   _____short courses
        ____Other (Please Specify):

    C. Are you interested in --
        ____half day programs   ____one day programs   ___two day programs
        ____Other (Please Specify):

    D. Are you interested in taking credit courses on a --
        Graduate level: Undergraduate level:
        ___MLS level   ___AA
        ___6th year degree/certificate   ___BA/BS
        ___Doctorate   ___School Media Certification
        ___Other (Please Specify):

III. A. <u>Administration</u>
      Financial Management
                      ____Budgeting
                      ____Fundraising
                      ____Grantsmanship
                      ____Other (Please Specify):

      Personnel Management
                      ____Affirmative Action/EEO
                      ____Compensation/Pay plans
                      ____Evaluation/Promotion/Dismissal
                      ____Selection/Interviewing
                      ____Staff Development
                      ____Total Quality Management (TQM)
                      ____Volunteer Management
                      ____Other (Please Specify:)

      Advocacy
                      ____Federal Legislature
                      ____Friends of Libraries
                      ____Library Trustees
                      ____Other Governing Boards
                      ____State Legislature
                      ____Other (Please Specify:)

      Planning
                      ____Buildings/Sites
                      ____Disaster Preparedness
                      ____Policies and Procedures
                      ____Program Planning
                      ____Role Setting
                      ____Standards & Accreditation

echnology - Networking & Information Retrieval

_____CD-Roms
_____Database Administration
_____Database Searching
_____INTERNET/NREN
_____Network Structures
_____OCLC Services
_____VA Library and Information
       Network
_____VA Public Education Network
_____Other (Please Specify:)

sues and trends

_____Access
_____Assessment of Programs/Services
_____Copyright
_____Distance Education/Learning
_____Downsizing
_____Economic Development
_____Electronic Publishing
_____Information Literacy
_____Intellectual Freedom/Censorship
_____Safety and Security
_____Other (Please Specify:)

ersonal Development

_____Communication/Interpersonal Skills
_____Customer Service
_____Public Speaking
_____Fitness and Health
_____Sensitivity Awareness
_____Stress Management
_____Time Management
_____Other (Please Specify):

nctions

_____Acquisitions
_____Basic Reference Tools
_____Cataloging
_____Children's Services
_____Collection Development
_____Electronic Access
_____Genealogy
_____Government Documents
_____Interlibrary Loan
_____Library Instruction
_____Marketing/PR
       Media

**Virginia Library Association. Continuing Education Committee
and the Virginia State Library and Archives**

_____The "One Person Library"
_____Preservation/Conservation
_____Reference Interviewing
_____Serials
_____Special Collections/Rare Books/Archives
_____Young Adult Services

F. <u>Other Topics (Please Specify):</u>

IV. Ranking of above choices
     List your top three choices:
         1. _____
         2. _____
         3. _____

V. Other comments:

VI. Please circle VLA Region where you work: 1 2 3 4 5 6
     (Map of Virginia with VLA regions detailed)

DEADLINE FOR RETURN *********Sept.15, 1993*********

RETURN TO: Nancy Newins
         Head, Library User Services
         McGraw-Page Library
         Randolph-Macon College
         Ashland, Va. 23005